ECOLOGICAL PSYCHOLOGY

ECOLOGICAL PSYCHOLOGY

Creating a More Earth-Friendly Human Nature

George S. Howard

University of Notre Dame Press

Notre Dame, Indiana

Manufactured in the United States of America

Library of Congress Cataloging-in-Publication Data

Howard, George S.
    Ecological psychology : creating a more earth-friendly human
nature / George S. Howard.
        p.   cm.
    Includes bibliographical references (p.).
    ISBN 0-268-00938-4 (alk. paper)
    1. Human ecology—Psychological aspects. 2. Human ecology—
Philosophy. 3. Nature—Psychological aspects.   4. Philosophy of
nature. 5. Overpopulation. 6. Consumption (Economics) 7. Human
behavior.
GF80.H69   1997
304.2—dc21   97-17527
                                                         CIP

∞ The paper used in this publication meets the minimum
requirements of the American National Standard for Information
Sciences—Permanence of Paper for Printed Library Materials,
ANSI Z39.48-1984.

As we face the wicked uncertainties of the twenty-first century, we do well to heed the wisdom offered by William James a century ago.

> We stand on a mountain pass in the midst of whirling snow and blinding mist, through which we get glimpses now and then of paths which may be deceptive. If we stand still we shall be frozen to death. If we take the wrong road we shall be dashed to pieces. We do not certainly know whether there is any right one. What must we do? Be strong and of a good courage. Act for the best, hope for the best, and take what comes. . . . If death ends all, we cannot meet death better. (James 1897, p. 31)

This book is dedicated to the memory of William James. His articulation of many of the philosophical beliefs that energize this book (namely, pragmatism, pluralism, radical empiricism, free will, faith, and strenuosity) makes our struggles to understand the world and human beings more fruitful enterprises.

CONTENTS

ACKNOWLEDGMENTS

Data found in Appendix A, Appendix B, and Appendix C were first published in Howard (1993a) and Howard, Delgado, Miller, and Gubbins (1993). Thanks is given to Sage Publications for permission to present those data here. Many colleagues, students, relatives, and friends were generous in their comments on earlier versions of these chapters. The feedback of Nancy Gulanick, my wife, was seminal in forming this book. Finally, my thanks go to Ryan Sweeney for inspiring me to pursue work in ecological psychology in spite of resistance to these efforts.

Part I

Think Globally

D O YOU BELIEVE that our world now faces an array of human-produced problems (e.g., global warming, ozone depletion, deforestation, desertification, acid rain) that threaten ecological disasters in the not-too-distant future? This book is the result of my personal journey from the discovery of an array of ecological problems that deserve our serious attention to the development of constructive changes in the ways we think and behave that will promote an earth-friendly human nature. The coming ecological crises are global in scope. Thus, we must first adopt a global perspective in order to understand their causes properly.

The first part of this book highlights the two general causes of our problems that emerge from the ecology literature—human overpopulation and overconsumption (or unsustainable lifestyles). Some of the material in Part I is depressing because the ecological threats are real and our time to act is shorter than many believe. I ask you to bear with this difficult examination of our earth's present condition as we must confront our situation honestly and realistically. However, our prospects are far from hopeless. We will examine dozens of ways that each of us might make the sort of lifestyle changes that will eventually reverse the troubling ecological trends that are now in motion. But we must first confront the hard facts of our problems honestly, to be certain that the solutions we initiate are more than mere window-dressing.

This book takes the perspective that there are a few important changes that can be made in the human nature that all of us have inherited at the threshold of the twenty-first century. These changes are necessary for our grandchildren to have a decent chance of inheriting an earth still capable of supporting a reasonable standard of human life. The understanding and modification of human nature (i.e., humans' thoughts, emotions, actions, and lifestyles) are necessary components in solutions to looming ecological difficulties, making psychology an important part of our multidisciplinary response to ecological challenges.

Several emotionally charged beliefs and issues will be challenged and analyzed in this book. Clinicians know that affect-laden topics must be considered many times and approached from many different perspectives in order to help clients to come to grips with the cherished beliefs that they would rather not subject to change via the light of reason. It is painful to question one's fundamental beliefs. Thus, the most important psychological points related to our savaging of the biological web of life on earth will be presented in a variety of ways.

Chapter 1 (On a Certain Blindness in Humans) identifies certain psychological blinders that enable us to avoid dealing with the ecological problems that lie close at hand. It is important to understand that these blinders serve important psychological functions, and thus we must attempt to replace them with care. The second chapter (Psychology and World Overpopulation) reviews some of the brute facts of global population trends. In Chapter 3 (Already Dead?) the important concept of carrying capacity is introduced and related to human population trends. Chapter 4 (Sustainability in an Increasingly Toxic World) makes the connection between carrying capacity and sustainability. Chapter 5 (The Business of Ecology) shows how businesses keep consumers from "doing the right thing" ecologically speaking. Simultaneously, consumers also keep businesses from "doing the right thing." Chapter 6 (Combating Killer Thoughts) demonstrates some of the current beliefs that serve to create and maintain the ecological problems we now face.

The mode of presentation of material in this book is inductive. The bases of ecological problems are first laid out. Then concrete, psychology-based responses to these problems are explained in Part II and the Appendices. Finally, a conceptual overview of the role that ecological psychology might play in the race to save our planet is presented in the Epilogue. However, readers possess a range of tastes in intellectual styles. For example, some readers prefer a more deductive presentation of material. For such people, first reading the Epilogue might provide the conceptual overview that they require to understand the place each chapter holds in the book's overall scheme.

Every psychologist has some model of human nature that undergirds her or his views of psychological topics and subsequent suggestions for change. Sigmund Freud saw a dynamic unconscious as the primary motivator of human actions; B. F. Skinner understood all behavior as attempts to maximize reinforcers and minimize punishers in one's life; Carl Rogers thought our lives represented carefully chosen strategies designed to actualize our latent potential as human beings. I believe there is some truth in each of these views. Further, biobehavioral factors such as enduring genetic influences and transient physiological states (such as those produced by drug use, sleep deprivation, etc.) also impact our actions. Finally, that cultural beliefs and social institutions (the government, organized religions, special interest groups, etc.) also influence our behavior is undeniable. Thus, one can see that my model of human action is complex and multifaceted. While space constraints preclude a systematic exposition of that model here, readers can consult Howard (1996), *Understanding Human Nature: An Owner's Manual* (cf., Chapter 4) for a detailed analysis of why humans act as they do.

Briefly, I see humans as self-determining, story-telling agents. While influenced by nonagentic causal factors (e.g., environmental influences, social pressures, biological factors), the heart of human action is self-determined (i.e., due to free will, volitionally produced, the result of agentic plans, desires, etc.). Further, our actions are largely constituted by the stories that we tell ourselves about what is real, true, and important in our lives. Each of us literally stakes his or her life on a small set of core stories about what is true and important in life. These stories are largely socially constructed, and the nature of their messages can be religious (e.g., Catholicism), economic (e.g., free market capitalism), political (e.g., liberal democracy), cultural (e.g., American rugged individualism), and so forth. The stories we choose to tell ourselves as foundational represent the primary motivation for creating the lives we live. However, nonagentic factors (e.g., social institutions, the beliefs of neighbors, the state of the economy) either facilitate or impede our efforts to create lives that are molded by the great stories of our time and place that we choose to believe are true.

This book will argue that some stories—that happiness comes through consumption of products (consumerism), or that organisms must strive to reproduce to the maximum (sociobiology)—

serve to stress the earth's fragile ecosystems. But by changing our beliefs, we can fundamentally remake the wellsprings of our human nature. Further, by carefully analyzing and deliberately remaking our social systems (e.g., tax laws, economic accounting principles), we can make it easier for all citizens to lead their lives in accordance with ecologically appropriate beliefs.

The human nature we have inherited from the nineteenth and twentieth centuries will prove toxic for the overpopulated world of the twenty-first century—which will be characterized by limited resources and overstressed waste sinks. Fortunately, human nature is somewhat malleable. Part I outlines some of the ways in which human thinking and actions might change in order to detoxify the human nature that we bequeath to our descendants in the twenty-first century. Finally, Part II, the Epilogue, and the Appendices represent concrete experiments that offer us real hope of becoming able to tread more lightly on our earth. What our beleaguered earth now needs most is a more earth-friendly human nature.

1

ON A CERTAIN BLINDNESS IN HUMANS

THIS CHAPTER'S TITLE is shamelessly stolen from William James (1899). The blindness of which James spoke, " . . . is the blindness with which we all are afflicted in regard to the feelings of creatures and people different from ourselves" (p. 232). Each of us is consumed by our own construction of reality—our fundamental beliefs, our plans, our hopes, and fears. It is only with effort that we come to recognize that one does not know reality itself, but only the reality revealed by our particular perspective. There are other perspectives to be considered—other realities to be probed.

James (1899) highlighted the fact that it requires special effort to come to understand the perspective and reality of an "other." In a famous example, James noted his horror at the sight of beautiful North Carolina mountains that had been newly cleared and planted, "The impression on my mind was one of unmitigated squalor. . . . The forest had been destroyed; and what had 'improved' it out of existence was hideous, a sort of ulcer, without a single element of artificial grace to make up for the loss of Nature's beauty" (James 1899, p. 233). But the scales immediately fell from James's eyes, as his "blindness" was cured by a single sentence from "an other,"

Then I said to the mountaineer who was driving me, "What sort of people are they who have to make these new clearings?" "All of us," he replied. "Why, we ain't happy here unless we are getting one of these coves under cultivation." I instantly felt that I had been losing the whole *inward significance* of the situation. Because to me the clearings spoke of naught but denudation, I thought that to those whose sturdy arms and obedient axes had made them they could tell no other story. But, when they looked on the hideous stumps, what they thought of was personal victory. The chips, the girdled trees, and the vile split rails spoke of honest sweat, persistent toil and final reward. The cabin was a warrant of safety for self and wife and babes. In short, the clearing, which to me was a mere ugly picture on the retina, was to them a symbol redolent with moral memories and sang a very paean of duty, struggle, and success. (pp. 232–234)

Each of us possesses his or her own inner world. The reality that we see and understand in the world around us is energized by the assumptions and perspectives, the values and biases, the twists and turns of our own inner world. As an observer of "that other," all one sees are the results of his or her inner world, as it influences the other person's overt behavior.

Freud (1936) noticed another important form of "blindness"— an intrapsychic blindness that he called denial. Denial is a defense mechanism in which a person protects himself or herself against a threatening thought (or impulse) by denying the existence of the threat (or impulse). Lazarus (1974) elaborates, "In the case of *denial,* the individual refuses to acknowledge a danger or a threatening impulse by asserting that it does not exist. He says 'I am not angry' or 'I am not dying of cancer' " (p. 472). Following the psychodynamic leads of Freud, Adler, and Fromm, Becker (1971, 1973) asserts that the denial of death represents the single most important dynamic in the formation of human personality. From this perspective, denial can be seen as a form of intrapsychic "blindness" that emerges from each human's struggle to come to grips with his or her own mortality. Perhaps the denial of death is (to greater or lesser degree for each of us) a fundamental aspect of our human nature. Similarly, this dynamic might also play a part in our discomfort in thinking about present population trends, their likely consequences, and what one might do to alter these alarming projections.

Similarly, Postel (1992), who sees the 1990s as the decisive decade for the planet and its inhabitants, targets denial and self-deception as the root cause of our problems.

Psychology as much as science will thus determine the planet's fate, because action depends on overcoming denial, among the most paralyzing of human responses. . . . This kind of denial can be as dangerous to society and the natural environment as an alcoholic's denial is to his or her own health and family. Because they fail to see their addiction as the principal threat to their well-being, alcoholics often end up destroying their lives. Rather than face the truth, denial's victims choose slow suicide. In a similar way, by pursuing lifestyles and economic goals that ravage the environment, we sacrifice long-term health and well-being for immediate gratification—a trade-off that cannot yield a happy ending. (p. 4)

At many points in this book I will describe terrifying, human-produced blights upon the earth (e.g., solid waste pollution, water pollution, massive deforestation, ozone destruction, desertification). There will be a strong urge to blame "others" who engineer this destruction, and who profit directly from the misuse and abuse of our natural world. Like James, we will be sorely tempted to lash out at the blindness and selfishness of these "others" who inflict scars upon our planet. But in their own inner realities, such people aren't trying to be destructive. They are just building a business, trying to have a little fun, providing a better life for their children, simply doing exactly what their parents did. We should all try to practice the charity suggested by James and attempt to be less blind to what these destroyers of the earth are trying to accomplish. I know of no one who would purposely set out to destroy the earth. However, all of us tax the earth's ecosystems (to a greater or lesser degree) as we undertake our daily tasks. One goal of this book is to raise our consciousness as to how *all of us* are unintentionally part of the human-produced ecological stresses that now threaten the earth.

One reason that raising awareness is important is because we perform many untoward acts precisely because we can't think of a good reason *not* to do them. Aerosol deodorants used to be a good example, as just a few years ago many millions of cans were sold each year. But then we learned that the CFC propellants were eating ozone molecules in the stratosphere at an alarming rate, thus subjecting all life-forms on earth to dangerous levels of ultraviolet radiation. Almost overnight the aerosol cans were gone. Now we are perfectly happy with roll-ons, pump sprays, or aerosols with benign propellants. For all those years as I raised my arm each morning I wasn't saying to myself, "I think I'll blast some stratospheric ozone." I was just blind to some of the consequences of my actions.

Another purpose of this book is to help readers to understand that their reason for performing a particular action does not exhaust the consequences of that act. This is because any action produces multiple effects—some expected and some completely unintended. When my wife and I decided to have a family, we never imagined that doing so would contribute to the global overpopulation problem—but it did, whether we considered it or not. Similarly, when an automobile manufacturer chooses to produce and advertise automobiles that get poor mileage, it is not for the purpose of producing more smog, carbon dioxide, and to make our country more dependent upon imported, nonrenewable, foreign oil than is necessary. Nevertheless, that is precisely what the manufacturing decision does. In the mind of the manufacturing company the decision was intended to meet perceived consumer preferences, or to increase the company's profit margin (since the profit margin on luxury autos is greater than on economy cars). Unfortunately for stressed ecosystems, whether an action was taken for "good" or "bad" reasons makes no difference, it simply adds additional stress. However, unless I am first aware of the relationship between an auto's gas mileage rating and its negative ecological impacts, I will never be able to let ecological considerations exert an appropriate impact upon my actions. Awareness is necessary for us to choose to do good things for good reasons. Thus, our blindness about the ecological consequences of our actions ought to be lifted by books such as this one.

Perhaps the most famous example of a group of individuals acting for "reasonable" motives, but producing catastrophic consequences is Hardin's (1968) *The Tragedy of the Commons*. In the original "Commons" example (where privately owned cattle graze on publicly owned grasslands and eventually destroy the public resource through overuse), greed by individual ranchers is the root of the tragedy. Many people who espouse an economic view of human nature claim that greed is good. However, greed in "commons situations" leads to many real world tragedies such as the decimation of North Sea herring fishing, the California salmon industry, and so forth. Still, greed is not always the root of our problems as Schelling (1978) and Willems (1974) convincingly show. The more general problem involves a focus upon individual goals and interests—or individualism (Bellah, Madsen, Sullivan, Swindler, and Tipton 1985; Sampson 1988), while failing to recognize that one's actions have multiple effects. Individualism tends to blind one to the reality that individual behavior also results in important group-level effects. Schelling (1978) gives a nice example of when each motorist who passes an auto accident on the side of the road slows to catch a five-second glimpse of the wreckage. This behavior can result in hour-long traffic tie-ups for thousands of motorists who happen to be behind them.

There is yet another human blindness—one that claims that our choices all come down to monetary considerations. Rational economic man theory offers this blindness as its fundamental assumption about human nature. Chapter 6 shows how many of our most cherished beliefs (e.g., the value of growth, progress, etc., the value of free market capitalism) spring directly from this maximization/optimization assumption. This presupposition alone produces tremendous ecological destruction. Replacing the blindness of the maximization vision of humans with more earth-friendly value systems (e.g., stewardship, sustainability) represents yet another ambition of this volume. I propose to show readers how we can begin the important task of making-over our human nature, in order to become a species that will not blindly destroy its only home.

The 1980s nurtured another interesting "blindness" concerning the relationship between ecologically appropriate acts and economically appropriate acts. Many politicians and business leaders opposed ecologically appropriate actions because *they assumed* that such acts would involve net economic costs. Every suggestion for ecologically appropriate reforms, it seemed, was stopped dead in its tracks with the response that the proposal would "cost American jobs." With further analysis, it became clear that this assumed, antagonistic relationship between ecological acts and economic outcomes was often wrong when only short-term consequences were considered, and almost always wrong when long-term consequences were calculated. Unfortunately, most individuals, businesses, and governments *heavily discount the future* (see Chapter 6) in their decision-making calculations. This, of course, is why the ecological projections and financial futures of so many individuals and nations look so utterly hopeless right now. We forget the wisdom of Shakespeare's warning to "Beware of what you desire, for you will surely have it." One who spends too much time consuming in the present has no future. Our blindness, as to how severely we discount future pain and happiness in our decisions, will be relentlessly attacked in this volume to help readers to understand how a proper respect for the future is a key element in a happy (and ecologically appropriate) lifestyle. Chapters 5, 6, 8, 10, and the Appendices will demonstrate in numerous ways how ecologically appropriate actions are also the most economically appropriate strategies to adopt, if one considers a time frame longer than the end of one's nose. The reality that ecologically wise acts are also economically helpful will become even more true in the world of resource scarcities, global overpopulation, and overtaxed waste sinks that will be commonplace in the twenty-first century.

Finally, have you noticed that my systems of valuing thus far have been completely human-centered? Our species' recent domination of the planet has severely imperiled many other life forms on the planet. The rate of nonhuman species' extinctions is currently running 1,000-times the typical rate of extinctions over the last several million years (Wilson 1992). This cataclysmic extinction is due to the world-wide human domination and destruction of natural habitats. We often give value to human wants and desires in our decision-making deliberations, but slight the interests of nonhuman species. Being less blind in this regard would be desirable if only because (ultimately) human survival is impossible without the web of life that supports our species. Savage that web, and we will surely kill ourselves. How blind can a seemingly intelligent species be?

2

PSYCHOLOGY AND WORLD OVERPOPULATION

THE HUMAN RACE is currently involved in a terrifying game of Russian roulette. But rather than having five empty chambers and one bullet, our deadly game involves many loaded chambers with the only uncertain element being how long present trends may proceed before they produce mass death. The loaded chambers might be labeled: ozone depletion leading to skin cancer; deforestation and desertification leading to starvation; chemical pollution of air, water, and food leading to suppressed immune surveillance and subsequent cancers; global overpopulation producing famine and war; and many other lethal possibilities. Must we continue to march like lemmings toward approaching ecological catastrophes? Or do we human beings have some degree of control over the future of our species?

Each year at Notre Dame, sophomores in an interdisciplinary course entitled "Ideas, Values, and Images" read Gore's (1992) *Earth in the Balance* to sensitize them to the enormity of the several ecological disasters that now threaten our planet. The book highlights the role of overpopulation as a common cause in all of these impending ecological catastrophes. A young woman in this course wrote an enlightening essay in response to class readings and discussions. The bulk of the paper represented a typical essay on the need for immediate action to forestall the various possible ecological disasters (ozone depletion, global warming, solid and gaseous pollution, water contamination, desertification, etc.). I quote the last two paragraphs in which she articulates her personal reaction to the impending ecological catastrophes.

What can I do to help the earth? I recycle newspapers, bottles, and aluminum cans. I do not use aerosols. I do not litter. But, these tasks involve no personal costs. I am surprised that despite all my new-found knowledge, I am not willing to sacrifice my personal happiness to save mankind. I am still going to have two children, or four, or six if I want. My first concern is not population control, but my own personal fulfillment. I do not care if neon signs flash in my face, my first priority is me.

People seem to fall into three categories: those rare few who will sacrifice all personal pleasure to save the world; those who deny the statistics; and those, like me, who know the state of the world, yet continue to live life as they wish with few personal costs. *Human nature impels us to deny our own impending destruction and to seek out happiness.* Of course, some people will help the environment to the best of their ability, but their own welfare always outweighs that of mankind. No matter how bright and loud the neon signs (statistics), society will continue to deny the impending end of humanity and will search for eternal satisfaction in the present. Our time on this earth is limited, and by our own human nature, we want to live a happy and successful life, even if that means the future destruction of mankind. Maybe the best course of action is not to *overly* concern ourselves with the environmental predicament but to enjoy life to the fullest, and let nature take its course. (Anonymous 1991)

In the paper the student offers a candid view into her personal world. We understand her personal vision of her future, and can imagine its implications for the future of our species. She is ecologically conscious and committed, but she is unwilling to curb her desire to have a large family. In fact, it is her belief that to do so would be contrary to human nature itself. What are the statistics on world population that this student feels that human nature itself compels us to deny?

The Population Bomb

It is very difficult to even imagine numbers in the hundreds of millions and billions. But the greater New York metropolitan area (including New York City, Long Island, parts of northern New Jersey and southern Connecticut) can provide a useful yardstick, because the population of that region (the United States' most densely populated area) will have remained virtually unchanged (at about 15 million people) from 1970 through 2000. While this region's population density will not have increased appreciably during that thirty-year span, the world's population during that thirty-year period will have increased (by conservative estimates, Brown 1991) by 2.55 billions of people. So while the New York metropolitan area's population will have remained unchanged over that thirty-year period, the remainder of the world's population has increased by the equivalent of *166 times* (16,600%) the population of the most densely populated part of the United States (or by about the number of people on the face of the earth in 1950!). While New York was the most populous metropolitan area on earth in 1970, by the year 2000 it will be surpassed in population (cf. Perlman 1990) by five cities (Mexico City, Sao Paulo, Tokyo, Calcutta, and Bombay). By the year 2010, projections have Shanghai, Seoul, Teheran, Rio de Janeiro, Jakarta, New Delhi, and Buenos Aires also surpassing the population of the still-stable New York metropolitan area. That our most densely populated area now appears rather stable (even though the population of the United States continues to increase) can present an illusory picture of what is occurring on the rest of our planet, where populations continue to grow at a terrifying rate.

Since the land area of "lifeboat earth" is functionally constant, population increases anywhere worsen the overcrowding of the planet and serve to exacerbate all of the resulting ecological problems (e.g., deforestation, desertification, global warming, famine, nonrenewable resource depletion, pollution). In this sense overpopulation is different from other aspects of general environmental deterioration, because it represents a *common cause* that contributes to deterioration in many other domains. Any lost ground to population inevitably translates into increased burdens on an array of the earth's ecological resources. Perhaps readers have heard news of declining birth rates and evidence of zero population growth in some regions for the early 1980s. I'm afraid that ray of hope has vanished also.

> Biologists find recent population trends profoundly disturbing. Accelerating sharply during the recovery period after World War II, the annual growth of world population peaked at about 1.9 percent in 1970. It then slowed gradually, declining to 1.7 percent in the early eighties. But during the later eighties it again began to accelerate, reaching 1.8 percent, largely because of a modest rise of the birth rate in China and a decrease in the death rate in India. With

fertility turning upward in the late eighties instead of declining, as some had expected and many had hoped, the world is projected to add at least *960* million people during this decade, up from *840* million in the eighties and *750* million in the seventies. (Brown 1991, p. 16)

What is most disturbing in research on population trends, however, is that books on population growth that were originally called "unrealistic" and "alarmist" (e.g., Ehrlich 1968) made specific projections (in the 1960s) about world population in the 1980s, 1990s, and the early twenty-first century. Remarkably similar projections for the 1980s, 1990s, and beyond were also made in the 1970s (cf., Tapinos and Piotrow 1978, who review projections by numerous independent groups). Demographic predictions currently being made for the year 2000 (and beyond) do not differ appreciably from those made in the 1960s and 1970s. Most disturbingly, it is now clear that virtually all of the population predictions made in the 1960s and 1970s for the last decades of the twentieth century have proven to be remarkably accurate. While accurate predictions represent an enormous achievement for the sciences of demography and population biology, they offer chillingly bad news for the human race. Human population trends are remarkably stable despite the fact that effective means of birth control (condoms, oral contraceptives, diaphragms, sterilization techniques, etc.) have been available since the 1960s.

Figure 2-1 depicts world population growth during the second millennium of our common era. The line creeps along low, almost flat, for centuries. Around A.D. 1000, it begins to rise slowly. Then in the twentieth century something startling happens: It shoots straight up. It took millions of years for the world's population to increase from a mere handful to a crowd of one billion. Adding the second billion took only 117 years; thirty-three years were required to accumulate the third; fourteen years produced the fourth and thirteen years the fifth. The sixth billion is due on board later this decade. I chose to present the more optimistic predictions for the future of population growth (in Figure 2-1) from the Population Reference Bureau (1989). The less optimistic Population Institute (1991) projected that we would reach ten billion people by 2028. Figure 2-1 gives one a sense of the trajectory of population trends

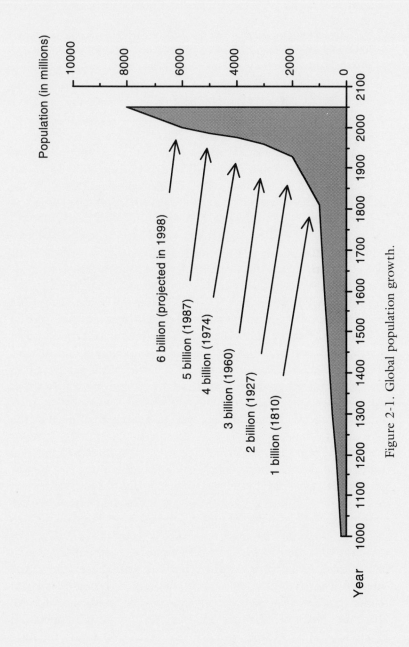

Figure 2-1. Global population growth.

and validates the first part of Malthus's (1798) seminal insight, that while population increases geometrically, food production increases only arithmetically.

While the data on the first half of Malthus's equation (population trends) look grim, what are the prospects for the full equation? That is, what is the relationship of population to food production? Catastrophic world starvation has been kept in check because of substantial increases in food production over the past two hundred years. Progress resulted from two sources: (1) technological improvements in agriculture; and (2) substantial increases in the amount of land in agricultural production. It is impossible to determine whether the agricultural improvements of the future will match the fabulous gains in productivity of our recent past. However, world trends in agricultural land use are now quite disturbing. As population increases, farmland is lost as towns and cities expand to house increasing populations. Further, overuse of farmland (along with water and wind erosion) makes farmland nonarable. Such problems lead to the disturbing realization that there has been a downturn in global per capita grain output, and that the world is probably past its peak in per capita grain production (as demonstrated in Table 2-1 which is reproduced from Brown 1991).

Between 1967 and 1990, Africa's per capita grain production declined by 28 percent. There is no reasonable prospect for reversing this trend in the foreseeable future. In a curious form of "blaming the victim," news reports claim that political instability produces starvation. The grain is there, the media claims, if only we could safely get it to the starving people. More likely, the truth is that famine leads to political instability—which is the reason that political chaos can be found wherever there is widespread starvation. Africa's future looks bleak. Table 2-1 also reveals that per capita grain production for every continent has peaked (typically in the early 1980s) and is now in steep decline. Other continents continue to have less and less surplus grain with which they can "bail out" Africa's starving millions. Does it surprise you that North America (the breadbasket of the world) reached its peak per capita grain production in 1981, and has declined by more than 12 percent since then? The world is close to complete utilization of arable land, so there is now little hope of replacing the vast quantities of land that become unfit

Table 2-1
Regional and World Grain Production Per Person, Peak Year
and 1990

Region	Peak Production		1990 Production	Change Since Peak Year[a]
	(year)	(kilograms)	(kilograms)	(percent)
Africa	1967	169	121	−28
E. Europe & Soviet Union	1978	826	763	− 8
Latin America	1981	250	210	−16
North America	1981	1,509	1,324	−12
Western Europe	1984	538	496	− 8
Asia	1984	227	217	− 4
World	1984	343	329	− 4

SOURCE: Based on U.S. Department of Agriculture, Economic Research Service, *World Grain Database* (unpublished printouts) (Washington, D.C.: 1990), with updates for 1990 harvest.
[a]Changes from peak year production always run the risk of capitalizing on statistical regression artifacts. However, regression problems should not be serious in these data, as the peak year almost always coincides with the point in which a positive grain trend (with respect to preceding years) turns negative (with respect to subsequent years).

for cultivation each year. However, many of us had naively believed that our cornucopia would go on producing forever.

A Bull Market for the Grim Reaper

Because psychologists are not accustomed to dealing with inexorable laws of nature, the following analysis of world population trends at first struck me as stark and oversimplified. The population of any species cannot increase indefinitely on our planet. Continued population increases coupled with relatively steady death rates (the current circumstance for the world) represent an inherently unstable situation. Either the world's birth rate *must* decline or the death rate will (of necessity) increase.

In summary, the world's population will continue to grow as long as the birth rate exceeds the death rate; it's as simple as that. When it [the world's population] stops growing or starts to shrink, it will mean that either the birth rate has gone down or the death rate has gone up or a combination of the two. Basically, then, there are only two kinds of solution to the population problem. One is a 'birth rate solution,' in which we find ways to lower the birth rate. The other is a 'death rate solution,' in which ways to raise the death rate—war, famine, pestilence—find us. The problem could have been avoided by population control, in which mankind consciously adjusted the birth rate so that the 'death rate solution' did not have to occur. (Ehrlich 1968, pp. 34–35)

Our inability to curb our birth rate demands increases in the death rate. The outline of how mortality will increase in the future is already taking shape. The World Health Organization now estimates that 40,000 children (i.e., less than five years old) needlessly *die each day*—that is, 14,600,000 such children die every year of disease, hunger, and neglect.

In the judgment of many, human overpopulation will be the root cause of enormous suffering and death in the coming century. Thus, population growth rates must be slashed immediately. Why, you may ask, is it critical that world fertility rates be curbed now— before we actually see ecosystems collapse under the strain of too many people? The answer lies with lag effects, which are apparent with all ecological problems. For example, in 1992 when rapid ozone depletion in the Northern hemisphere was documented, many were stunned to learn that even if all production of chlorofluorocarbons (CFCs) had ceased immediately (a virtual impossibility), ozone depletion would still continue into the twenty-first century due to CFCs already in use and in the atmosphere. If the world's current fertility rate of 3.6 children per family was somehow instantly, miraculously reduced to the replacement-level fertility rate of about 2.1 children per family, the world population would *not* level off at its present level of almost 6 billion. One-third of the population of our planet is now fifteen years of age or less. Thus, the child-bearing years of many people *are just beginning*. Even if a replacement-level fertility rate was somehow miraculously achieved and maintained for the next thirty years (with present death rates remaining constant) the population of the earth would increase by two billion people—eventually leveling off at around eight billion people (cf., Tapinos and Piotrow 1978) due to lag effects. This chill-

ing, demographic certainty underscores the need to drastically reduce fertility rates immediately—before the collapse of various ecosystems become imminent.

What are we to make of the quick (but perhaps quite perceptive)
claim by the sophomore (quoted above) that one group of people
employs denial to distance themselves from the spectre of world
overpopulation—in her words, "those who deny the statistics"?
People who employ that defensive strategy would probably have
thrown this book aside in annoyance before they finished the statistics on world population and food trends. Such people might have
convinced themselves that the population numbers are inaccurate,
and that the general tone of the discussion reflected the political
biases of the author.

My spring 1996 course in "Ecological Psychology" helped me to
compose and edit an article that appeared in the April 13, 1996
edition of the *Chicago Tribune*. Because the article tied global overpopulation to declines in food stocks, most of the letters we received
angrily denied our population figures and their connection with declines in grain stocks.

Food Can't Keep Pace with Population

Notre Dame, Ind.—A March 30 *Tribune* Business article bore terrible news: "Corn futures and cash prices soared to the highest levels in history after the government reported stocks have dwindled
to the lowest levels in nearly 60 years, prompting concerns of summer shortages."

This news rang a bell for me because nine days earlier, in *The
New York Times,* I learned that the March wheat contract closed
out more than 18 percent higher than any wheat contract in history—an ominous sign.

In the *Times* article, futures traders predicted that wheat contracts will go even higher because of " . . . strong demand out of
Asia, wheat stocks at their lowest level in more than 20 years, and
reports that as much as 60 percent of the current winter wheat crop
is in poor to very poor condition with the central Plains region
having its driest winter in a century."

We can ignore the last reason given for the current wheat crisis.
Yearly fluctuations in production represent a transitory factor; there
will always be better than average and worse than average crops.
Strong demand for wheat out of Asia should surprise no one, how-

ever. This spring our world must feed almost 100 million more people than last spring. Much of this growth occurs in Asian countries. The Earth's population will again increase by another 100 million hungry mouths by next spring.

The bottom line is that worldwide grain demand will only increase for the foreseeable future, unless we control worldwide popuation growth. Because the United States' grain surpluses cannot match the soaring grain deficits of the rest of the world, grain stocks are being drawn down all over the world. This is how record crops can still fail to stem the depletion of food stocks such as wheat. Reversing this worldwide food deficit represents an almost impossible task if we continue to add to the globe's population by almost 1 billion people each decade.

The current food situation is like a business that racks up losses year after year. Unless losses are reversed, the business must eventually go broke. The world is now living unsustainably with respect to food. In 1960 the World Health Organization estimated that more than 40,000 children (less than 5 years old) needlessly die each day. These children are overwhelmingly the victims of starvation and the diseases that prey on the malnourished. Of these 40,000 daily deaths, two-thirds of the children fail to make it to their first birthday. Unless current, worldwide population and food trends are dramatically changed, we will inevitably have worldwide starvation that will dwarf all previous famines.

Unfortunately, when that happens newspaper headlines will probably again mistake symptoms for real causes. We will talk about "demand out of Asia," "depleted stocks" and "drought in our central Plains." We will see the victims as suffering from bad luck when in reality they will be paying the price of our denial that overpopulation ensures that all Four Horsemen of the Apocalypse—war, strife, famine and pestilence—will ride fast and hard in the 21st Century.

George S. Howard

Discussions of the role that political ideologies played in ecological discussions dominated many of our class sessions. We had anguished over the left-leaning tone of an earlier draft of the *Chicago Tribune* article on food and population. However, we eventually realized that the term "conservative" had multiple meanings. Some of the early twentieth-century American conservatives (e.g., Teddy Roosevelt) based their political views on the need to conserve and protect what was valuable in our political traditions. This was a parallel process to their work to conserve wildlife through the expansion of our system of National Parks. Conversely, another strain of American conservatism finds great value in the *status quo,* and thus is instinctively skeptical of all suggestions of change. From the conservation perspective, the food and population article above can be seen as a paradigmatically conservative piece. Thus, overall, the class felt that they had helped to craft a balanced, ideologically neutral, factual statement.

A week after the article appeared an anonymous letter arrived that bore only a post office box number in Hobert, Wisconsin. Inside were four professionally produced pamphlets entitled "World Population Facts," "Total Fertility Rates Are Plunging Worldwide," "The World *Can* Feed Its People," and "More Grain on Less Land." These pamphlets were accompanied by a scribbled note that simply said "Chicken Little—the sky is *not* falling." The four pamphlets' messages were quite consistent with one another. If anything, we have to worry about there being *too few* people on our earth—not too many. Further, gains by modern agriculture will be more than able to meet global food demand. Consider this quote from "The World *Can* Feed Its People" pamphlet, "world grain production increases will need to slow[!] if huge stock accumulations are to be avoided . . . " (exclamation point in original). Of course, the disparity between our "facts" and the "facts" trumpeted in these pamphlets was quite unsettling to the students. Which side was telling the truth? Who was lying?

A senior (who was also a native of Wisconsin) took it upon himself to find out how the pamphlets' authors could see the world population situation so differently than the picture depicted in Figure 2-1 of this book. The first few lines of the "Total Fertility Rates Are Plunging Worldwide" pamphlet gives the flavor of their message.

> Throughout the world birth rates and total fertility rates are plunging faster and further than ever recorded in human history. Despite all the apocalyptic doomsday predictions of certain over-population propagandists, the fact is that population growth in many countries are already below replacement levels and the world's growth rate is rapidly approaching that figure. . . .

By the end of the pamphlet a naive reader might be convinced that our species' real threat is this "plunging fertility" problem, not overpopulation.

Our intrepid senior shed light on these (seemingly) conflicting data by constructing a table based upon data found in *World Population Monitoring, 1992* (New York: United Nations, 1994), p. 30.

During the years	Annual Growth Rate (percent)	Annual Increment (millions per year)
1965–1970	2.1	72
1975–1980	1.7	74
1985–1990	1.7	88
1995–2000	1.6	98

These data show that the pamphlet was technically correct in that the annual growth rate *is* declining—in fact, it has been declining since about 1965. But this fact should not allay our fears of over-population in the slightest. The last column shows that we continue to break the record for *increases* in the human population year after year after year—with no prospect for this trend reversing in the foreseeable future. The mathematics of these *apparently* incompatible truths is really quite simple. Compare the years 1965 with 1997 to see how compatible declining annual growth rates can be with an out-of-control, geometrically increasing human population:

1965: 3.3 billion (Population) × .021 (Growth rate) = 70 million
people annual increase
(births minus deaths);
1997: 5.9 billion (Population) × .0165 (Growth rate) = 92 million
people annual increase
(births minus deaths).

Our class realized once again how easy it is to lie with statistics. Earlier in the semester the students had seen similar statistical sleights-of-hand when their politicians had trumpeted "a decrease in the rate of growth in the national debt." Put much credence in that kind of "good news" and you'll surely have a smile on your face as you are shown the way to the poor house.

I didn't share with the class my thoughts on the truly dark side of these misleading pamphlets. The writer(s) of these pamphlets were enormously sophisticated as mathematicians and demographers. (They even made a sophisticated argument that 2.26 was the proper children-per-woman value for the replacement fertility rate, rather than the commonly cited value of 2.1 children per family.) Anyone with that much sophistication in these domains must know that he or she is producing *disinformation* that serves to obscure the truth about what clearly are troubling overpopulation trends. Such people (while technically correct) are intellectually dishonest (in my opinion). Why would anyone want to convince me and my students that there is no danger in overpopulation, when the danger is so obvious and so real?

The pamphlets reminded me of a wonderful quote that tied overpopulation to the sorts of blindnesses that were described in Chapter 1.

> The emerging history of population is a story of disaster and denial—disaster foreseen, but disaster psychologically denied in our innermost being. Our reaction to the signals assaulting us is perfectly understandable: they foretell an event that has never happened before. How can one believe in something—particularly an unpleasant something—that has *never* happened before? This necessity must have been a terrible problem for Noah. Unfortunately the Bible is silent about Noah's psychological experience, surely the most significant aspect of his ordeal. If it was wisdom that enabled Noah to believe in the never-yet-happened we could use some of that wisdom now. (Hardin 1964, p. vii)

Incredible wisdom will be required for our species to consciously reverse biological evolution's most basic commandment—that we reproduce to the maximum.

Whatever their logic, many people generate reasons to deny the threat inherent in the trends identified above. But the student whose essay opened this chapter assigned herself to a different group, "those, like me, who know the state of the world, yet continue to live life as they wish with few personal costs. Human nature impels us to *deny* our [the species'] own impending destruction and to seek out [individual, personal] happiness." Italics and bracketed material were added to her quote because I believe the psychological dynamics she describes in herself do not represent denial (as psychologists understand it), but might better be described as self-deception

(Lockard and Paulhus 1988). The bracketed material highlights my belief that in her quote, "our" refers to an horrific outcome for the human species, whereas by the second set of brackets she is thinking of the happiness of individuals. She deceives herself into believing it is reasonable to expect that an individual can achieve happiness in the midst of a group that is experiencing a tragedy.

The economist Thomas Schelling's (1978) analyses (using examples, such as a traffic jam, interracial housing, etc.) show how an entire group of people, each of whom behaves for the sake of the same, reasonable *individual* motivation, can produce a group-level outcome that all of these people find abhorrent. The sophomore, quoted above, is a product of American individualism and the "me generation" thinking of the 1970s and 1980s. From that perspective, it appears to fly in the face of human nature *not* to seize the course of action that meets her individual needs (i.e., to have as many children as she desires). But if the student possessed a more ecological worldview, she would be more disposed to see the group-level effects of her individual choices, and to value actions that benefit both her *and* the species. Thus, she might think something like the following, "Human nature dictates that we not act in a way that further endangers our species (like having many children) as the future quality of life of all—myself included—is diminished by overpopulation." That this hypothetical thought might appear to some to stretch credulity (more than her original thought that humans always act in their own self-interest) speaks to the need to develop more compelling, ecological worldviews.

The average woman (worldwide) now gives birth to about 3.6 children over her lifetime, while 2.1 children per woman would represent a replacement fertility rate. Suppose, for cultural or religious reasons, women *insisted* upon having four rather than two children. Mathematically it is true that a woman who has four children beginning at about age thirty-six exerts far less population pressure on the earth than a woman who has only two children, but who begins having children at age eighteen. If parents start families later in life, it can benefit the earth and its ecosystems as much or more than if families actually reduced their families' sizes. A quick thought experiment will clarify this counterintuitive thought. (See Figure 2-2.)

Imagine a woman (G_0 in Figure 2-2 top panel) who has two chil-

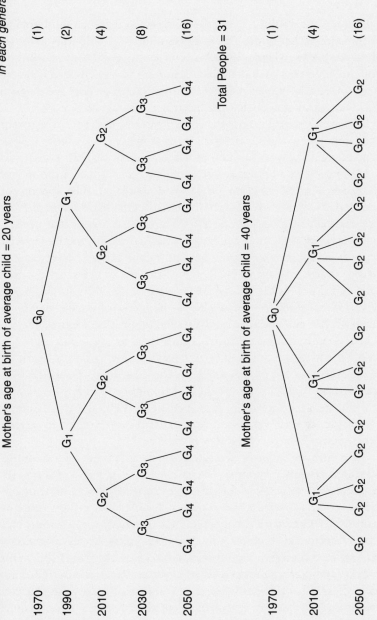

Figure 2-2.

dren rather early in her life. Her first child might have been born in 1988 (when the mother was eighteen years old) and the second child born in 1992 (when the mother was twenty-two years old). Assume also that all her progeny will exhibit her same fertility pattern (i.e., two children, early births). The column on the left side of the figure gives the date of birth of the mother (G_0) and the average date of birth of all children in each subsequent generation (G_1, G_2 . . .). The righthand column presents the number of people in each generation. In this hypothetical example, in the year 2052 the fifth generation would be complete and a total of thirty-one people would be represented in this family tree.

The lower panel of Figure 2-2 is identical to the top panel except for two important changes. First, instead of having a below replacement level fertility rate of two children per family, the mother (and all her descendants) will have four children per family. Second, we also double the mother's age at the time of birth of her average child. For example, the G_1 children might have been born in the years 2008, 2009, 2011, and 2012. In this instance, the family tree of people who have larger families later in life total only twenty-one members by the year 2052. This demonstrates the counterintuitive reality that efforts directed toward having people delay their child-bearing years can be even more helpful than efforts to reduce family size.

While Time Is Short, There Are Reasons for Hope

The thrust of this chapter was that human population trends are ominous for the ecology of our planet—and because the population's growth rate is geometric, our time to act is short. That reality notwithstanding, there are some reasons for hope, because all global trends are not negative and some negative phenomena actually produce positive side effects. A few examples might prove instructive:

First, while global population increases geometrically, total fertility rate (i.e., the number of children per woman) worldwide has been declining since about 1965—although it is still far in excess of the replacement fertility rate.

Second, while global warming will likely turn some currently arable sections of the world into deserts, other regions (e.g., parts of Canada, the former Soviet Union) will likely increase their crop yields due to longer growing seasons and higher carbon dioxide levels in the air.

Third, while per capita grain production continues to decline worldwide, there are tremendous inefficiencies in our food distribution systems. Food scarcities will likely lead to improved technologies of food production (e.g., agricultural biotechnology) and distribution, if necessity still remains the mother of invention.

Fourth, because it takes ten vegetable calories to produce one meat calorie, the ratio of calories of vegetables to calories of meat in humans' diets will probably increase as food scarcities get worse. This sort of change in Americans' diets might even have salutary health benefits.

While other examples of possible positive side-effects of otherwise negative trends could be given, all serve to dramatize the reality that ecological issues are extremely complex and multifaceted, defying simplistic analysis and solutions. While there might be some silver linings to current ecological trends, on balance the trends appear ominous to the overwhelming majority of scientists who study them carefully.

3

ALREADY DEAD?

FORMER UNIVERSITY OF Southern California football coach John McKay used this story to depict the unshakable self-confidence of his buddy, Alabama football coach, Bear Bryant. As McKay told the tale, he and Bear were duck hunting when a lonely mallard flew over their blind. Bear took dead aim on the solitary traveler and blasted away. The duck flew toward the horizon as if unaware it had even been in harm's way. Bryant turned to McKay in utter disbelief and stammered, "John, do you see that? Thar flies a dead duck!"

Bryant's image of an already-dead duck still flying into the future returned to me one Valentine's day when an article entitled, "Ecosystems Identified as Critical or Endangered" reported,

> In the first full review of the health of the American landscape, a new federal study has concluded that vast stretches of formerly vibrant natural habitat, once amounting to at least half the area of the 48 contiguous states, have declined to the point of endangerment.
>
> Although the plight of individual species has been the focus of public interest, the health of the larger interconnected community of plants, animals and microbes of which they are a part—the ecosystem, nature's functional unit—is perhaps more important as a gauge of vitality. The new report finds that scores of ecosystems, of widely varying types and sizes, have declined on a grand but largely unappreciated scale. If the remnants should vanish, say the study's authors, species adapted to them would probably vanish as well. (Stevens 1995, p. A5)

The shift in emphasis from endangered species to endangered ecosystems is important because it can help us to turn away from distracting arguments like: Is it more important to save the spotted owl or a handful of logging jobs for a few more years? Given the enormity of the global problems awaiting us at the dawn of the twenty-first century, spotted owl–type debates amount to fiddling while Rome burns. So what evidence points to looming catastrophes? Here the notion of crashing ecosystems enriches our thinking.

My colleagues in ecology tell me that an ecosystem is like a boat, and the various species in that ecosystem are like the passengers on the boat. During our planet's several–million–year history there have been at least five periods of widescale crashing of ecosystems, and resulting extinction of many species. The last episode occurred at the end of the Cretaceous period, about one hundred million years ago when a sudden catastrophe, perhaps a meteor striking the earth, produced climatic changes that destroyed numerous ecosystems and resulted in the loss of thousands of species, including the dinosaurs. (See E. O. Wilson [1992] *The Diversity of Life,* chaps. 10 and 11 for a lucid description.) Returning to the analogy of ecosystems being like boats, the Cretaceous catastrophe was like the Titanic striking an iceberg—many species (passengers) perished while others survived in altered but still viable ecosystems (lifeboats). However, the ecosystem collapses that might soon confront us will likely be of a very different sort.

I believe the question, "How many people can live on the face of the earth?" represents the most important question of our age. Who is equipped to answer such a question? Certainly not psychologists—so don't look to me. Clearly, the question lies outside the realm of expertise of politicians, environmental activists, business leaders, and a host of other "interested" parties in this debate. Professional ecologists are the people whose training enables them to best answer the question of the *carrying capacity* of the earth. But before we hear ecologists' verdict on this issue, let's review some relevant facts.

Humans occupy virtually all of the habitable land masses of the earth. Will the total land area of the earth change over the next 100 years? If global warming is a reality, all models predict that several portions of the earth (e.g., south Florida, parts of Louisiana, Bangladesh, areas of India, several Pacific islands) will be lost to human habitation due to rising oceans. However, technological advances might make a few currently uninhabitable areas (e.g., Arctic and Antarctic wastes) suitable for humans. [I personally don't care to live there, but you're certainly welcome to do so.] So, for the purposes of this analysis, let's be conservative and conclude that the available land mass will remain roughly constant.

Measurement in science ranges from cases which are "virtually certain" (e.g., measurements of time, weight), through instances that are "extremely well supported with small errors in measurement" (e.g., the current population of the earth), down to estimates with "large uncertainty in measurement present" (e.g., measures of personality traits, determining an ecosystem's carrying capacity). Except for the projections of future population levels in Figure 2-1, only highly reliable and valid measurement estimates are made for the years 1000 A.D. to 1995. While one might quibble over the exact population values depicted for any recent year in Figure 2-1, even if a challenge to these numbers proved to be correct, it would result in a trivial change in the graph and no change in the interpretation of the graph. For example, suppose someone objected that the 1994 population estimate of 5.64 billion (and adjacent values) overestimated the earth's true population by 150,000,000 people (which is an extremely unlikely possibility given the precision of modern demographic techniques). If this unlikely suggestion were proven true, the solution to the problem would be to move each of the values (i.e., years) on the x-axis less than two years to the left. Consider Figure 2-1 closely, do you think anyone could even detect whether these x-values were offset by two years? Would any such change seriously alter our conclusion about the trend toward global overpopulation? All it would mean is that there are two more years than we previously thought before the earth's population reaches (or has already reached) some extremely important levels—namely, its carrying capacity and its maximum capacity.

Human population is a key to all the pressing environmental issues we face—it represents a common element in all the threats that earth's ecosystems face.

> The size of the human population affects virtually every environmental condition facing our planet. As our population grows, demands for resources increase, leading to pollution and waste. More energy is used, escalating the problems of global warming, acid rain, oil spills and nuclear waste. More land is needed for agriculture, contributing to deforestation and soil erosion. More homes, factories and roads must be built, occupying habitat lost by other species that share the planet, often leading to their extinc-

tion. Simply put, the more people inhabiting our finite planet, the greater the stress on its resources. (Weber 1992, p. 1)

Contrast the precision of the population data in Figure 2-1, and our confidence in its meaning, with the scientific evidence for global warming. First, our current measurement strategies for obtaining average global temperatures are comparable in precision to the measurement of global population. However, we have good evidence that at several points in history the earth's average temperature was *higher* than current temperature levels, and that enough ecosystems survived these temperatures without troubling levels of loss of species. Stated slightly differently, while it is almost certain that the average global temperature has been rising over the past century, this trend might still be due to longer-term swings in global temperatures. Further, it is far from clear that increasing temperatures pose a significant threat to human life and the ecosystems needed to support human life on our planet. The scientific evidence still allows for substantial disagreement as to the causes of recent temperature increases and the significance of the impact of such changes for ecosystem integrity. Examples of such reasoned disagreement are typical (and also healthy signs) for active areas of science.

In spite of the fact that science never proves anything conclusively, there are numerous instances where a very firm consensus emerges after periods of lively debate. For example, cigarette smoking has been reliably linked to lung cancer—the consensus within the scientific community is solid on this fact. However, because science cannot prove anything beyond doubt, one can still assert that it has not been proven that smoking causes cancer. Some people (quite incorrectly) use that fact to assert that cigarette smoking does not lead to lung cancer. Such people are wrong in drawing that inference and are espousing scientifically implausible positions. While such positions might be interesting for what they imply about the political commitments, financial interests, or psychological defenses of their advocates, they are substantially at variance with the clear consensus in the scientific community on the evidence available today.

The scientific status of global overpopulation is closer to the status of the "smoking leads to cancer" debate than it is to the global warming debate. It is clear that the size of the human population is increasing at an alarming rate. Unlike the global warming scenario, there are two chances that at some point in history the earth supported a human population of six billion or more with minimal damage to ecosystems—those chances are infinitesimal and none! Thus, we are now sailing dangerous, uncharted waters. Even if some incredible scientific discovery in the future leads us to believe the world once was home to a population of around six billion humans, something must have killed off billions of them to achieve a population of about 100 million around 1000 A.D. So we would hardly be encouraged by that miraculous discovery—even if it were to occur. In short, it is hard to imagine how a responsible reading of the human population record can give anyone cause for optimism. People who see little reason to worry (after reviewing the trends toward human overpopulation) probably reveal more about their psychological defenses than they reveal about the scientific merits of the issue. [As we say in my profession: It's got long legs, feathers on its butt, and its head is buried in the sand. If it isn't an ostrich, then you tell me what it is!]

Of course, human fertility might decline on its own due to the pressures of an increasingly overcrowded world, changes in sexual behavior due to AIDS, and so forth. However, as discussed in Chapter 2, even if human birth rates decline precipitously, this decline could be too little, too late. This point is clarified further when we recognize ecology's enormous difficulties in estimating the maximum capacity and the carrying capacity of our planet.

The maximum capacity is the population that an ecosystem simply cannot tolerate, as the ecosystem that supports human life will simply collapse. However, the more critical value is the (always smaller) *carrying capacity:* the population size that an ecosystem can sustain indefinitely. Once an ecosystem's carrying capacity has been exceeded, the too-large population is maintained (for a time) by overtaxing the resources of the ecosystem. This situation is similar to a business that runs a series of yearly losses which over time erode the company's net asset value and eventually lead to bankruptcy. Evidence of ecosystem deterioration is like a series of yearly business losses. Continued losses suggest there are serious structural problems in a business, just as continued, widespread ecosystem deterioration might suggest that the human population has already exceeded the earth's carrying capacity. People who refuse to do anything about the size of the human population until some catastrophe (e.g., ecosystem collapses and the resulting devastation) forces them to act are like executives who will not acknowledge that their business is in trouble until they are involuntarily forced into bankruptcy. Companies that will not respond to continued losses are doomed long before that reality is forced upon them. As Bear Bryant might say, "George, do you see that balance sheet? Thar goes a business in liquidation."

Given that it is such an important number, what do ecologists think is the carrying capacity of the earth? Unfortunately, that value cannot now be assessed with precision due to the relative immaturity of the science of ecology, and a number of special measurement difficulties in assessing any ecosystem's carrying capacity. For example, ecologists must assess a moving target, as current technological advances in farming, water processing, and the like will undoubtedly change the earth's carrying capacity. Hence, ecologists' estimates are speculative with broad bands of uncertainty in measurement and imprecision readily acknowledged. Witness the fact that some ecologists believe the planet's human carrying capacity has already been exceeded, while others see eight billion souls as a critical level. Whatever the true value, our present practice of increasing the earth's human population by more than 90,000,000 (total births minus deaths) *each year* is taking an unjustifiable risk with the one and only home our species will ever know.

Earlier I implied that the potential anthropogenic ecosystem collapses of the near future will be of a different sort than the Cretaceous period extinctions. Rather than the "Titanic striking an iceberg" analogy, a more realistic image sees humans deciding to ignore the carrying capacity of our planet, and allowing our population to grow until ecosystems collapse, before acting. Consider a parable about an overloaded lifeboat to highlight the notions of sustainability and carrying capacity in discussions of global population. Imagine that a sinking ship had only one usable lifeboat, and that the ship held far more passengers than the lifeboat could accommodate. The lifeboat's manufacturer indicates that it can be safely occupied by thirty adults (its carrying capacity). Should only thirty people be allowed aboard? Given the gravity of the situation, some might argue that allowing forty on board is justified. However, we know that there is some finite number where the addition of that last person will swamp the lifeboat—killing everyone (its maximum capacity). Surely we would *not* choose to add people until the worst occurs.

However, the issue is even more difficult because the lifeboat might be able to handle (for example) sixty people when it is partially sheltered alongside the sinking ship. Unfortunately, it might be the case that once outside the ship's protection, the wind and waves would immediately sink a lifeboat with sixty people aboard. That is a problem for people who view the current world population as "proof" that earlier apocalyptic projections (such as by Paul Ehrlich in 1968) as having been "disproved." Like the sixty grateful people pushing their lifeboat away from the sinking ship, at our current approximately 5.9 billion souls we might already have passed the earth's sustainable population level. We simply might lack the foresight and understanding to realize that as a species we are already dead. However, since no one knows the earth's exact carrying capacity, there may yet be a bit more time left for us to act.

My research specialty is the psychology of free will (i.e., self-determination, personal agency, or volition). After centuries of heated debate, it is now clear that individual humans possess a reasonable degree of ability to choose and self-determine the course of their lives. This has been shown when the impact of all nonagentic causal influences on their actions has been methodologically controlled. While this power to self-determine one's actions is now demonstrated beyond reasonable scientific doubt (at the level of the individual), it is not at all clear that humans as a species possess a similar capacity to manage the course of their collective future. If our species lacks the power to control its size, then our future looks grim indeed. I still believe we can (to some extent) choose the destinies that we and our children will experience. But we must first learn to heed present warnings if we are to have time to avert horrific futures.

I had a disturbing nightmare recently. In the dream, God and Bear Bryant were passing the time of day somewhere in the cosmos when the earth flew past them as it traced its heavenly orbit. They exchanged sad glances, for they suspected that our human population had already exceeded the earth's carrying capacity. Sadly, Bear said, "God, do you see that? Thar flies my already-dead species."

4

SUSTAINABILITY IN AN INCREASINGLY TOXIC WORLD

THIS CITY IS usually hot in the summer. It's not uncommon for the temperature to break 100 degrees for brief periods, and high humidity levels are also commonplace. However, six weeks ago, midday temperatures hovered around 100 degrees for five straight days accompanied by high humidity levels. Life was difficult for everyone; for over 700 people life was snuffed out. Most victims were buried within a week. The final forty-one unclaimed bodies of victims were all buried yesterday. Places like Somalia, Bosnia, and Rwanda recently have taught us that societies in disarray will often produce victims whose identities are untraceable. So where did these victims of the heat live? Calcutta? Manila? Jakarta? Teheran? São Paulo? No, this time the victims were residents of Chicago during the summer of 1995.

Feeling sorry for the Chicago victims is easy. Understanding why this event occurred, and deciding if it is a harbinger of worse tragedies to come, is extremely difficult. For example, is this further evidence of the breakdown of order in our cities? Might it be an early warning of many crises that will be precipitated by global warming? Or is it further evidence of our society's devaluing of all human life?

I was writing my presidential address for the Division of Humanistic Psychology of the American Psychological Association when the news of the forty-one unclaimed, Chicago victims arrived. In that address, I explain that humanistic psychology takes no official position on the existence of God, in the hope that both theists and nontheists will feel welcome. Unlike Secular Humanism, which holds that human beings represent "the ultimate good," humanistic psychology holds that humans represent one (among several) important "goods." Thus, the overwhelming majority of humanistic psychologists are theists of a variety of belief systems. Humanistic psychology sees human life as a very important "good" that is now facing many severe threats. The challenge of my presidential talk was to convince that audience of sophisticated theists/humanists how too many "goods" (i. e., people) can produce an intolerable evil.

Overpopulation Kills Also

Pro-life advocates oppose abortion because they say it kills human beings; ecologists oppose human overpopulation because it kills members of many living species (humans included). Demographers and ecologists tell us that for each life lost to abortion, dozens (perhaps hundreds) of human lives will be lost in the coming decades due to the effects of human overpopulation. Why are volumes devoted to abortion, and virtual silence on the lethality of overpopulation, if the latter is a much more devastating killer? In *Living within Limits: Ecology, Economics, and Population Taboos,* the ecologist Garrett Hardin (1993) claims that society now colludes in a massive cover-up designed to never speak a specific truth—that overpopulation kills! According to Hardin, that last sentence violates a very strong population taboo and thus engenders anger, suspicion, and defensiveness in many people.

You already know my views on overpopulation. However, overpopulation is only half of the story of why we are now close to many ecological tragedies. The other half of the picture involves the overconsumption (or unsustainable lifestyles) by many people in the developed countries. Did you know that even if the world's current population doubled to 11.8 billion, we would not strain our planet's ecosystems any more than we now do, if every human simply cut his or her standard of living by 50 percent? We can have more people if all of us are willing to dramatically lower our standard of living. [Of course, people already at the subsistence level can't reduce their living standard much further without dying, so the rest of us will need to reduce our lifestyles by more than half in order to achieve that 50 percent reduction in lifestyles overall.] Thus, the best hope we have of keeping our present lifestyles, and raising hundreds of millions of citizens in underdeveloped countries slightly beyond their current subsistence levels, is to stabilize (or lower) the human population. If not, nature will simply inflict a "death rate solution" upon us in whatever way nature sees fit.

Sustainability

In Chapter 3 we discussed an ecosystem's carrying capacity. The impact of a human population and its activities on an ecosystem can be determined by the following formula (see Ehrlich and Ehrlich 1991):

$$I = P \times A \times T$$

The formula I = PAT is read as: The impact (I) of any group can be understood as the multiplication of the size of its population (P) with its per-capita affluence (A) as measured by consumption, that then is multiplied by a measure of the damage done by the technologies (T) employed by supplying each unit of that consumption.

When a population's total impact (I) exceeds the ecosystem's carrying capacity, the ecosystem begins to deteriorate. Unless the human impact is soon reduced, an ecosystem pushed beyond its carrying capacity will deteriorate until it eventually crashes. Counting the number of humans in a population is a reasonably straightforward task, so determining the value P in our I = PAT formula is relatively easy. Measuring the population's affluence level is much more difficult, as it is problematic to combine entities like land, water, air, energy, etc. into one overall measure. The ecology literature has found that a population's measure of energy consumption serves as a good surrogate for a population's level of affluence given current technologies (AXT). This is because several disparate entities (e.g., forests lost, oil burned, food consumed) can be converted into energy unit equivalents with little distortion, and because the amount of waste produced by these activities is highly correlated with the amount of energy consumed in the activity.

The technology (T) term is often mistakenly thought to signify an anti-technology bias in the I = PAT equation. The T-value simply reflects the environmental *destructiveness* of the techniques used to produce the goods and services consumed. In fact, more sophisticated technologies can produce either higher T-values or lower T-values. For example, complex technologies, like nuclear-powered electric plants, can have high T-values because we cannot now safely deal with radioactive wastes for the thousands of years that they require attention. Similarly, chlorofluorocarbons (CFCs) used as aerosol propellants, cleaning detergents for microprocessors, and for heat transfer in cooling units used to be considered low-T commodities. But we discovered that CFCs were also greenhouse gases (which raised their T-value somewhat), and then their T-value went off the scale when we realized that these CFCs were rapidly destroying the earth's ozone layer which protects us from the sun's ultraviolet rays.

Chapter 7 describes a program to replace technologically simple incandescent light bulbs with more sophisticated compact fluorescent light bulbs. These more technologically advanced bulbs have much *lower* T-values because they consume far less electricity to produce a given quantity of light. Thus, a given population can maintain the same level of affluence (use the same quantity of light) but reduce their environmental impact by almost 80 percent simply by using the more benign (i.e., lower T-value) compact fluorescent bulbs rather than continuing to employ the technologically simple (but very wasteful) incandescent light bulbs. Chapter 5 discusses exactly how businesses and government might cooperate to alter the price of destructive technologies in order to help consumers make ecologically correct purchases, rather than selecting the usually cheaper, wasteful technologies.

Money Games and Sustainability

Wasteful products now tend to be priced artificially low due to the current practice in economic accountancy of *not* factoring all of the product's real costs into its market price. The net effect of this practice (of externalizing some real costs) is to either dump these ignored costs on society in general (i.e., Hardin's CC-PP game: to communize costs but privatize profits) or to postpone paying that debt until it falls to some future generation to clean up the mess. All of these economic sleights-of-hand allow society to consume (and waste) more in the present, while erroneously thinking that the "fair market cost" of the goods or services in question cover all the real costs of the product. By ignoring the deterioration done to our soils, bodies of water, atmosphere, etc., by current business practices when calculating the price of consumables (e.g., food, electricity, paper), we live unsustainable lifestyles that destroy the one-time-only gift of our natural world by a handful of overpopulating and overconsuming generations.

My generation might well be remembered as the one that developed a system of economic accountancy that raised gluttony and theft to an art form. In addition to the practice of externalizing costs during the closing decades of the twentieth century, my generation made unbalanced budgets and the amassing of debt almost as natural as breathing for our governments and households. Debt accumulation represents another form of an unsustainable lifestyle that passes inappropriate burdens on to the next generation.

In subsequent chapters our corrupt practices of ecological accountancy and our current personal (and governmental) monetary practices (e.g., assuming debt, refusing to save money) will be examined. These practices follow from the same defensive psychological prejudices (i.e., self-deception and avoiding realistic accountability) that lead us to severely overweigh *present* costs and benefits relative to *long-term* costs and benefits in the calculus of our decision-making processes. Furthermore, our economic and ecological futures are directly linked to one another in that financial assets represent an important *resource* for creating sustainable lifestyles. If our country did not have an almost $5 trillion national debt, we would have about an extra $700,000,000 *each day* to use to fight ecological problems and develop a more sustainable society. Unfortunately, that $700 million daily buys us *nothing*—it simply goes to service our collective indebtedness.

If your household is now financially solvent, you can purchase some of the aids (described in Chapters 7, 8, 11, and 12) to reduce your family's T-value, and thus lessen your impact (I) on your ecosystem. If your family is deeply in debt, your free money goes toward servicing your debt, rather than purchasing energy-saving devices and building a sustainable future. Chapters 10 and 11 painstakingly document how to correct habits of indebtedness and how you might begin to become financially solvent again. Because the United States is the world's largest debtor, its ecological future looks far grimmer than you might imagine if you had not realized the ways in which debt makes achieving sustainable lifestyles doubly difficult.

Ecologists and environmental economists, stress the importance

of the five biological principles of sustainability—conservation, recycling, renewable resource use, restoration, and population control.
As Chiras (1995) notes,

> If you could reduce the environmental crisis to its basics you would
> find that it is here because, for the most part, we do not use re-
> sources efficiently. Nor do we recycle much or restore damage to
> vital ecosystems. Our use of renewable energy is, for the most part,
> pitifully inadequate, as are our measures to control population
> growth and urban sprawl.
>
> The biological principles of sustainability could form the basis
> of a long-term proactive strategy that fosters lasting solutions,
> avoiding costly cleanups or end-of-pipe solutions or expensive spe-
> cies recovery plans. Their economic potential is enormous. In most
> cases, sustainable solutions provide the same service as conventional
> approaches, but at a far lower cost. They also tend to employ many
> more people than traditional approaches. And, making them even
> more appealing, sustainable strategies provide far better environ-
> mental gains than traditional approaches. (pp. 204–205)

Readers interested in exploring the biological principles of sustainability further should study Ehrlich and Ehrlich (1991) or Chiras
(1992). This book will provide some specific examples of ways of
living a more sustainable lifestyle in several domains (e.g., waste reduction, reducing energy consumption) and discuss a number of
interesting psychological implications of these actions.

The Problem of What's Good for Individuals *versus* Collectives

Can there be a healthy tree in a sick forest? There certainly can
be—in the short run. However, in the long run, whatever it is that
is killing the rest of the forest's trees will probably overtake the currently healthy individual tree. For a variety of reasons late-twentieth–
century humans have turned their attention and concern away from
the health of the collectives of which they are members and focused doggedly upon their own health as individuals. Robert Bellah
and his co-authors (1985) claim that the first language of American
moral life has become *self-reliant individualism*. There are second
languages that we also know—the languages of tradition and commitment. However, these second languages are called into use *only*
"when the language of the radically separate self does not seem ade-

quate" (pp. 20–21). In the first language of self-reliant individualism, one need not even worry about the health of the rest of the forest—it is enough to know that the individual tree is doing fine. However, in the second languages, the health of the community represents a *precondition* for any individual to be healthy. My college class' twenty-fifth anniversary reunion will be held a few months from now. If I asked every classmate, "How are you doing financially?" they'd all think of their (individual) assets if they chose to reply to my impolite query. Would anyone even think to reply in the second language and say, "Terrible! We're almost $5 trillion in debt!"? Exactly how valuable will your wealth (e.g., stocks, bonds, insurance policies, homes) be if we (collectively) go bankrupt?

Can a Child Grow Up Healthy in a Toxic Environment?

Too much human activity can pollute (e.g., garbage, liquid wastes, carbon dioxide) a physical environment. But humans live in more environments than just their physical environments. My family, my job, my local community, and my nation also represent social environments in which I live. Can a social environment also be polluted?

James Garbarino (1995) in *Raising Children in a Socially Toxic Environment* wrote, "What I mean by the term *socially toxic environment* is that the social world of children, the social context in which they grow up, has become poisonous to their development" (p. 4). Social toxicity is meant to parallel the physical toxicity that now threatens the survival and well-being of many biological species. Garbarino then identifies,

> the social equivalents of lead and smoke in the air, PCBs in the water, and pesticides in the food chain. They're easy enough to identify: violence, poverty and other economic pressures on parents and their children, disruptions of relationships, despair, depression, paranoia, alienation—all of the things that demoralize families and communities. (pp. 4–5).

"Not to worry," I thought, as I read the characteristics of a toxic social environment. "My kids aren't depressed or alienated. Nor are they the victims of violence, or drugs, or a broken home, or bad schools, or . . . " And then I caught myself. I was thinking individualistically. Sooner or later our toxic social environment will extract

a toll on all children—mine included. Can a healthy tree go un-
scathed in a dying forest?

Garbarino then depicts how much more dangerous it is to grow
up in the 1990s than it was for him growing up in the 1960s.

> When I was in high school in the 1960s, I used to write an opinion
> column for the school newspaper. One month I wrote an article
> criticizing the fraternities at my school, an act that angered many
> of my peers. As a result, late one night a car pulled up and dumped
> garbage on the lawn of our house: I was the victim of a drive-by
> *littering.*
>
> Today, in many communities, the consequence of making your
> adolescent peers mad at you might be a drive-by shooting instead
> of a pile of garbage on your lawn. The same behavior that thirty
> years ago produced a rather benign form of intimidation might
> today get you killed. This insight started me thinking about the
> many ways in which the social environment for kids today is more
> dangerous than it was when I was growing up. *Drugs:* There was
> no crack cocaine available to troubled kids then. *Violence:* It was
> almost unheard of for a teenage bully to have a gun. *AIDS:* We
> were warned off sex, but no one said we would die from it. *Televi-
> sion:* The content of television programs was bland and innocuous
> by today's standards. *Family instability:* Most families had two par-
> ents and could afford to live on one income.
>
> These thoughts led me to the concept of the socially toxic envi-
> ronment, the idea that the mere act of living in our society today
> is dangerous to the health and well-being of children and adoles-
> cents. (Garbarino 1995, pp. ix–x, emphasis in original)

Do you know how metaphors work in science? Neils Bohr used
our understanding of the sun and the planets in our solar system to
help scientists imagine what the relationship of the atom's nucleus
and its electrons might be. For over fifty years, Bohr's model of
the atom served as a scientifically fruitful metaphor. In a metaphor,
a scientist takes a well-accepted or well-understood phenomenon
(e.g., the structure of our solar system) and invites other scientists
to increase their understanding of a poorly understood phenomenon
(e.g., the structure of the atom) by noting similarities between the
two. Garbarino feels that the ecological decline and toxicity of our
physical environment is so apparent, well understood, and accepted
that it can serve as the base metaphor for the emerging toxic social

environment with which our children must also deal. Parts of this book deal with concrete ways that we might strive to arrest the decline and increasing toxicity of our physical environment. Such decline must be halted before we can begin to think about paths toward sustainable development. The definition of sustainable development is: development that meets the needs of the present without compromising the ability of future generations to meet their needs (Schmidheiny 1995). Thus, halting deterioration in our environment represents the first step (a precondition) before sustainable development can become a possibility.

Garbarino (1995) points out that we are short-changing our children by asking them to grow up in socially toxic environments (e.g., crime, drugs, family instability), just as we are short-changing them by leaving them a degraded, toxic, physical environment. Improving the social and physical environments in which our children will develop will require both more money and greater commitment of our time and energy. Sadly, these demands come at a time when societal pressures and our current lifestyles make money and time extremely scarce commodities for most adults. However, if we do not soon break current trends and invest more time and money in our children, we will have squandered our other (along with our planet) most important natural resource.

This chapter began with the story of forty-one unclaimed bodies of victims of the heat in Chicago. At that time I claimed that understanding why this event occurred, and deciding if it was a harbinger of worse tragedies to come was extremely difficult. Then I asked, "Is this further evidence of the breakdown of order in our cities? Might it be an early warning of the crises that will be precipitated by global warming? Or is it further evidence of our society's devaluing of all human life?" Since this is a book on the breakdown of the physical environment, I'll bet many of you initially thought that I felt that global warming was the "correct" explanation. But now we can see that all three causes might be implicated in the Chicago tragedy. The breakdown of the physical and social environments are, in my judgment, closely related contemporary phenomena. Garbarino (1995) correctly observes that the highest price to be paid for these sins will fall disproportionately heavily upon the people who are least able to defend themselves from these increasingly more toxic environments—our children.

5

THE BUSINESS OF ECOLOGY

BEING RESPONSIVE TO the earth's ecological needs is often very frustrating for businesses. In the ecology literature, business and global overpopulation are routinely vilified as the primary causes of the many problems that threaten to compromise human life on our planet. However, research in ecological psychology reveals how businesses are sometimes victimized when they attempt to solve the ecological problems that they have been accused of having created. A brief example of how this can occur might prove illuminating.

GE's Problems in Bringing Good Things to Life

For all of its wonder, Thomas Edison's incandescent light bulb is tremendously inefficient. About 90 percent of the energy consumed produces heat rather than light. Compact fluorescent light bulbs give the same amount of light, using only 20 to 30 percent of the electricity that incandescent bulbs require. Shifting from incandescent to compact fluorescent bulbs would save consumers 70 to 80 percent of the lighting portion of their electric bills. In addition, people who spend more money for air conditioning than they do for heat would also reap lower net energy bills, as the high heat levels produced by their incandescent bulbs would not have to be overcome by air conditioning.

Light bulb efficiencies would *not* be an ecological issue if our electricity came from nonpolluting, renewable energy sources such as solar, tide, geothermal, or wind power. However, since nonrenewable, polluting energy sources (e.g., coal, oil, natural gas) supply the lion's share of the fuels that produce our electricity, light bulb inefficiencies are important ecological issues. Recognizing this fact, GE and other companies (e.g., Sylvania, Osram) have developed and aggressively marketed compact fluorescent bulbs. In spite of the fact that compact fluorescents are in the best economic interests of consumers (and the best ecological interests of our world) for the past ten years they have been a tough sell in the United States. Admittedly, earlier versions of the bulbs had several unattractive features that limited their appeal to consumers. Present versions are greatly improved, however, and are quite acceptable. Still, market penetration has been very limited. While I have thirty-four compact fluorescent bulbs that are working hard to save money and electricity in my home, I've never seen more than two in anyone else's home. Have you seen significant numbers of compact fluorescents in anyone's home?

Compact fluorescents generally last 10,000 hours, whereas incandescents last 750 to 1,000 hours. Thus, one compact fluorescent lasts as long as ten to twelve incandescent bulbs. Using nationwide average costs, the materials cost for a compact fluorescent is $20 versus a conservative estimate of $7.50 (10 bulbs × .75 per bulb) for comparable incandescents. However, the electricity cost for a compact fluorescent is $20 (25W × 10,000 hrs. × $.08 per kW. hr.) versus $80 (100W × 10,000 hrs. × $.08) for comparable incandescents. Thus, the total cost of lighting is $40 for the compact fluorescent versus $87.50 for equivalent incandescents. So why do you have so many incandescents and so few compact fluorescents in your home?

Most of the subjects in my research projects report that they have never heard of compact fluorescent bulbs. Yet, to its credit, GE is aggressively marketing them. Rarely a day goes by that I don't see a television ad for GE's compact fluorescent bulbs. (Have you seen the ad where a kid asks his friend, Tommy, "How many grown-ups does it take to change a light bulb?" Reflecting upon the durability of compact fluorescents, Tommy wonders, "Why would anyone need to change a light bulb?") Given GE's barrage of advertisements, it's strange that so many research subjects claim they have never heard of compact fluorescents. One wonders if people would buy them if they had heard of them.

In studies conducted at Notre Dame, we found that fewer than one in four people buys a compact fluorescent even after: a) learning of its ecological and economic benefits; b) receiving a one-week free trial with the bulb; and c) being offered a 20 percent price discount. If only one in four buys under those circumstances, how will we ever get substantial numbers of consumers to pay full price when they consider compact fluorescents on store shelves?

Shortsightedness—Thy Name Is Human!

As a child, I used to rush through every task—it was just part of my nature to do so. My father would stop me dead in my tracks as he chided me in his slow, Southern drawl, "Slow down, boy. Life's a distance race, it's not a sprint." How right he was! The more one studies ecology, the more one learns that it is the long-term vision that is important. Short-term considerations are not nearly as important as they initially might seem. The more one studies psychology, the more one realizes that humans *almost always* sacrifice important long-term considerations to trivial short-term rewards or punishments. It's our credit card lifestyle, the "live for today—don't sweat tomorrow" mentality. When asked whether they'd prefer to receive $16 now or $20 a year from now, most Americans take the money and run. In doing so, they turn down a guaranteed, tax free, 25 percent rate of return on their investment! Now how smart is that? This is an example of how people *discount the future*. Ornstein and Ehrlich (1989) argue convincingly that we have evolution to blame for our self-defeating preference for short-term thinking. Regardless of where this self-defeating, short-term outlook comes from, our challenge is to find ways to help people to behave in ways that produce good, long-term consequences.

The task for psychologists (and for GE and ecological activists) is to train people to prefer superior economic and ecological options over cheap, temporary need-satisfiers in the calculus of their decision making. Consider the following question as we begin to understand the lines of thinking that lead so many people to self-defeating choices. Is buying a light bulb more like buying a can of tuna fish or buying a share of stock?

If your gut reaction is that it was more like buying a can of tuna, then you are probably imagining yourself as a *consumer* in framing your choice between the incandescent or compact fluorescent bulbs. Consumers see themselves as having a "need"—for food, light, a car, etc.—which they try to satisfy at as low a cost as possible. If you need a can of tuna, you survey the range of prices for brands of tuna that are "good enough" for you, looking for one that might represent a "bargain." If purchasing a light bulb is similar (in your mind) to buying tuna, then that $.75 incandescent "bargain" will get you every time.

Conversely, when you buy stock you should not think like a consumer, you should think like an investor. Investors consider likely *rates of return* on their investments, and they also tend to think in longer time-frames than do consumers. Using the figures calculated earlier, and assuming a light bulb is in use for fourteen hours per day, the $20 investment in a compact fluorescent would yield $47.50 in savings in less than two years. That represents a guaranteed, tax-free, annual rate of return of almost 60 percent! Would any shrewd investor turn down that offer? Well, millions of us routinely do so.

The sad truth is that human shortsightedness maintains the needless waste of 70 to 80 percent of the electricity used for residential lighting today. GE and several other companies stand ready to sell us either highly efficient or very wasteful lighting devices. GE shareholders will be happy to know that the company's profit on one compact fluorescent is about the same as on ten incandescent bulbs. Thus, GE's fiduciary responsibility to its shareholders is satisfied whether or not customers choose the ecologically appropriate option. Yet, because we all care for the future of our planet, I would not be surprised if GE would be pleased if compact fluorescent sales dwarfed incandescent sales, instead of the current, opposite circumstance. Thus, in this case, American business is *not* the cause of this ecological difficulty. If any blame is to be assigned, it should be placed at the feet of shortsighted, consumer-oriented humans. We have met the enemy—and they are us!

It's as unfair to lump all ecological activists together as it is to lump all businesses together. Some environmental activists would not be pleased with me for placing blame with American consumers (and away from business) in the above example. But the theoretical divisions among ecologists go deeper still. For example, some (e.g., Glendinning 1995) see society as gripped by a social pathology called "techno-addiction." The road to societal recovery lies in rejecting our technology-dominated lives, and slowly returning to a simpler way of life. From that perspective, a problem created by a relatively simple technology (such as an incandescent bulb) should *not* be cured by a more complex technological device (a compact fluorescent bulb), since more complex technologies move society even further in the wrong direction. Universal agreement about appropriate steps to solve ecological problems cannot be achieved—even among ecological activists. With that thought in mind, I'd like to present a general model that might be applied broadly to the many business-related causes of ecological deterioration. While not an infallible cure for ecological difficulties, the strategy can profitably be employed to lessen many ecological strains in a very business-friendly manner.

The Greening of the IRS

This cryptic heading suggests an answer to the riddle, "How can we initiate new taxes, but pay no more in taxes?" An answer might be by initiating "green taxes" that will replace dollar-for-dollar our federal income taxes. First, what is a green tax, and why is it a business-friendly way to ecological sanity?

Capitalizing upon your new knowledge of the finances of light bulbs, imagine that a green tax of $.10 was levied on the sale of all incandescent light bulbs (whether produced domestically or abroad). The cost is immediately passed on to the consumer, who now pays $.85 per bulb. Thus, GE's profit margin is unchanged. Consumers pay no more in total taxes because federal tax rates are lowered to produce income tax savings equal to the total of all green taxes collected. Thus, a consumption tax replaces an income tax dollar-for-dollar to produce no net change in taxation. As with sales taxes, business collects green taxes, which moves the IRS a bit further from our lives. Paul Hawken (1993) claims that if we took green taxes seriously, we might put the IRS completely out of business. Wouldn't that be a pleasant, indirect outcome!

The green tax on incandescent light bulbs would rise to $.20 in the second year, $.30 in the third year, and so on until the twentieth year, when the final green tax level of $2 per bulb would arrive. By then, we would almost all be converted to compact fluorescents because, at over $2.75 per bulb, who would prefer incandescents to compact fluorescents? Light bulb companies continue to earn the same profit, but now it comes from the sale of efficient technologies rather than wasteful technologies. The twenty-year phase-in period enables all light bulb companies the time to make whatever adjustments are necessary to adapt to the changing market conditions produced by the green tax.

Everyone knows that the income tax serves as a disincentive to earning, saving, and investing. If $10 billion were raised in green taxes on incandescent bulbs over a twenty-year period, then $10 billion in disincentives would be removed from our income tax bills. However, there are known problems with all consumption taxes, and such problems will need to be worked out for any green taxes. But whereas other consumption taxes are crude—like saturation bombing—green taxes work with the precision of "smart" bombs. If we taxed *all* light bulbs (presumably because they are involved in producing pollution), the supply-demand laws suggest that people would buy fewer lightbulbs—thereby cutting corporations' profits. With a green tax on incandescents, consumers will (in the longer run) spend a smaller percentage of their income on lighting, while corporate profits from light bulbs still go essentially unchanged.

Some industrial problems require an even finer-grained approach to green taxes. Instances where a good product–bad product distinction does not fit so easily require a more nuanced approach. For example, electric utilities use many energy sources to generate power (e.g., hydro, coal, natural gas, solar, oil). Rather than coarsely labeling some as "good" and others as "bad," a more precise tailoring of taxes would better serve our national interests. A panel of environmental experts might rank-order the various fuel sources with respect to many factors (e.g., amount and types of pollutants, domestically available–imported, renewable-nonrenewable), yielding the following relationships with respect to the undesirability of each fuel source:

Source Undesirability:	Coal			Wind
	Oil	> Natural gas >	Hydro >	Solar
				Geothermal
Maximum green tax:	100%	50%	25%	00%

The lower line indicates the percentage of some maximum level of green tax to be placed upon each energy source of electricity. Thus, the price of nonrenewable, polluting, imported fuel sources would increase dramatically. Conversely, renewable, nonpolluting, domestic sources would pay no green tax. Again, such taxes might be phased-in over twenty years, and the trillions of dollars raised would lead to enormous reductions in the federal income taxes we pay. The problem of ozone depletion (caused by chlorofluorocarbons) might have been solved via green taxes rather than the phased-in bans that were employed. Similarly, the ratio of fuel efficient to fuel inefficient cars on our highways could also be increased via green tax solutions. If you would like to read more about the political, social, or economic feasibility of green taxes, please see Paul Hawken's *The Ecology of Commerce* (1993).

Free Markets: Reality or Fiction?

Do green taxes represent unwelcome intrusions into the actions of our free marketplace? Perhaps to the surprise of many readers, my answer is "Absolutely not!" I'd argue that our present markets are not free and properly functioning *precisely because all* of the real costs of our goods and services are *not* included in their market prices. Green taxes would allow us to enter real costs (e.g., the price of emitting greenhouse gases; producing acid rain; depleting nonrenewable resources; destroying natural habitats) into market prices. The destructive consequences of our business practices are currently being treated as *externalities*. Green taxes allow us to internalize these externalities, and thus would produce, for the first time, a complete, truly free market that might then work its wonders. This true form of free market capitalism would not destroy our planet, as the current free-market-impostor form of capitalism is now doing.

The renewable, efficient, and nonpolluting technologies that will dominate the twenty-first century cannot compete in a marketplace that will not fairly charge inefficient, polluting, nonrenewable competitors for their negative impacts. In the light bulb example, because GE's sales and profits continue to come from their more wasteful, polluting product (i.e., incandescent bulbs), GE is virtually mandated not to move more aggressively in pushing the efficient technologies that we need to solve our ecological crises.

During the 1992 global environmental summit held in Rio de Janeiro, our Japanese and European competitors openly declared their belief that, "the development of energy efficient technologies represents the largest potential market in the history of the world." Because the prices of gasoline and electricity in Japan and Europe are far higher than they are in the United States (due to taxes that sometimes act like green taxes), American companies now possess a slight, short-term competitive edge. But these same American companies are crippled in their struggle to develop the technologies of efficiency *because* our energy costs are now kept artificially low. I fear that the long-term competitiveness of American business is now being sacrificed at the altar of a short-term competitive advantage.

As this book goes to press, the 1993 pump tax of 4.3 cents per gallon on gasoline is being repealed (with the support of *both* political parties). The following essay was Faxed and E-mailed to about eighty colleagues around the country. I urged them to also share the essay with their students.

Gutless Wonders

Each semester I ask students in my Ecological Psychology class to identify the most effective piece of environmental legislation in the 1990s. No student yet has mentioned my choice—the 4.3 cents gasoline tax. If the law of demand still operates, any price increase will reduce demand somewhat—exactly how much depends on the relative price elasticity of the commodity. Less gas used means less pollution, less reliance on foreign oil, a lower trade deficit, and a slight competitive advantage for fuel efficient automobiles relative to gas guzzlers.

When the Clinton administration adopted the gas tax it was also billed as an effective deficit reduction move—and it was! Thus, repealing the tax demands that the government cut spending to compensate for the approximately $5 billion per year in lost revenues. Will we now stiff education, national defense, welfare, crime prevention, or some other domain in order to replace these lost revenues? Since both Clinton and Dole are rushing to take political credit for repealing the gas tax, it is obviously not a partisan issue. Rather, both parties see this as a way of currying favor with the electorate. The worst we can accuse the politicians of this time is following public opinion, instead of leading it. Then who are we to blame for slaying what is arguably the best economic and ecological idea of the 1990s?

Who are the gutless wonders who are now killing a goose that has faithfully laid golden eggs for us year after year? It's you and me. Unless we rise up in unison and scream, "Anyone who touches that gas tax is my lifelong political enemy," the tax is a dead duck.

The instant either party believes that 51% of the electorate favors the gas tax, Dole and Clinton will leave footprints on each others' backs scrambling to take credit for being the tax's staunch protector. A courageous politician would stand behind a solid policy when only 40-something percent of the voters/consumers realized that it is in our best long-term interests to now pay a few cents more at the pump. But I've heard that political courage midway through an election year represents the leading cause of dead political careers.

Let's at least be honest enough to admit that it's all of us who will pull the trigger that kills the gas tax. Perhaps this time we won't scapegoat the politicians for merely doing the will of the people. So contact the candidates. Express your opinion. Or forget that old notion of a government of the people, by the people, and for the people.

George S. Howard

Clinton telephone
202-456-111

Dole telephone
202-224-6521

I gave copies of the essay to the class on May 9th and asked the class if they would make every effort to change the minds of our politicians. Most students volunteered to help and later gave me verbal summaries of their efforts to convince a few friends and relatives to call their elected officials and urge them to keep the gas tax.

It was easy to demonstrate the ecological importance of the 4.3 cent gas tax to my students because they understood the concept of green taxes. While technically not a green tax, the gas tax acts in a similar manner by suppressing demand for an ecologically inappropriate commodity.

Our low cost of energy stimulates greater overall energy consumption. Is it any wonder that we, as Americans, are responsible for 60 percent of the world's energy consumption (and subsequent pollution)—even though we have but 10 percent of the world's population? Green taxes would be an excellent first step toward rectifying our overreliance on cheap energy. Such taxes would immediately make clean, renewable, energy-efficient, alternative technologies more cost-effective. The prospect of gradually increasing green taxes over the next two decades will enable American businesses to pursue the technologies of efficiency more aggressively, as we quickly phase-out the inefficient, polluting technologies of the twentieth century. Finally, as business collects more and more green tax revenues, we will approach that glorious day when we might say, "Remember the bad old days, when we used to have to pay income taxes . . . "

6

COMBATING KILLER THOUGHTS

THE TITLE OF the book *Mind as Healer, Mind as Slayer* (Pelletier 1977) suggests the theme of this chapter—while some thoughts might heal, other thoughts can kill. Wisdom is being able to distinguish the killers (or toxic thoughts) from the healers. The craft of living lies in populating ones' thoughts and activities with healing beliefs while minimizing the use of killing thoughts. The list of thoughts presented herein does not exhaust the domain of killer thoughts (see Ellis 1994, chap. 4, for a very different list). The nine mistaken beliefs I identify are killer thoughts that particularly threaten our ecological future. Other toxic thoughts, such as, "War is an effective method of settling disputes," are more toxic for human life and happiness than they are for the environment. Thus, I do not deal with them here.

In *The Battle for Human Nature,* Schwartz (1986) demonstrates that three important contemporary belief systems—rational economic man theory, behavioral psychology, and sociobiology—represent slight variations on a common theme. Each applies the same basic idea to a different content domain of human action. First, utility maximization is assumed to drive human actions for most contemporary economic theory. Similarly, human action is seen by behavioral psychologists as attempts by people to maximize reinforcements while minimizing punishments. Finally, in sociobiology, actions are seen as the result of attempts by "selfish genes" to maximize the number of their kind that make it into the next generation's gene pool. I will argue that this behavior maximization/ optimization theme represents a vision of human nature that will spawn many killer beliefs for the twenty-first century.

However, Herrnstein (1990) correctly observes that belief in the maximization/optimization vision of human action now represents our most basic, unexamined assumption about human nature. Thus, it will probably be difficult for many readers to hear arguments against such basic beliefs as the value of our current so-called "free market" capitalism. The high levels of resistance that greet challenges to any human's core beliefs need to be approached carefully. Thus, an example of a toxic, killer thought that readers might have an easier time in understanding and deploring will be considered first.

Table 6-1 presents nine killer thoughts that result from our current maximization/optimization view of our human nature. Since the beliefs sketched in Table 6-1 will lead to overconsumption by affluent people (and nations), they thus have become toxic. Notice that when these thoughts developed, in the underpopulated world of the nineteenth century, they were quite appropriate for that world of one to one and a half billion people (where the Industrial Revolution was just gaining momentum). However, these thoughts will be quite dangerous for a twenty-first century (of eight to twenty billion people) characterized by overstressed waste sinks (e.g., polluted air, rivers, oceans, landfills) and crashing ecosystems. Furthermore, although I want to introduce these killer thoughts to you at this point, these ideas will become more specifically clear and applicable as you read the chapters in Part II of this book.

Table 6-1
Killer Thoughts: For a World with Limits

1. Consumption will produce happiness (and consumption is "needed")
   - I'll be happy when I get that new Lexus, my home on the beach, etc.
   - Shopping as a form of relaxation; catalog shopping; The Shopping Network
   - The belief that if consumers stop buying, then people will lose jobs
2. The future is to be steeply "discounted"
   - We are the "Now generation," so we don't need to think (or worry) about the future. We'll "worry about that later"
   - Buy now—make no payments until next year (as individuals given a line of credit, or as a nation with an enormous national debt)
3. Present consumption is preferred to investment in (or conservation for) the future

- Short-term rewards and punishments are greatly overvalued relative to long-term consequences in the calculus of decision making
- No one speaks for the rights of the next generation (i.e., draining the Social Security Trust Funds)
- Debt is now as natural as breathing

4. Growth is good
   - GDP must always increase
   - An undeveloped resource is a wasted resource
   - More of a "good" (e.g., people, products) is preferred to less

5. Free-market capitalism is the best system
   - "Greed is good"—we should all get as much as we can
   - The CC-PP game (communized costs–privatized profits)
   - Systems should *encourage* greater human economic activity (throughput)

6. Paying less (for something) is better than paying more
   - Cheap gas (or electricity, or water, etc.) is preferred to expensive commodities regardless of their real, total costs
   - Keep prices as low as possible by externalizing whatever costs possible
   - Government support for "commons situations" (e.g., leasing federal land for grazing) is a great "deal"

7. If it ain't broke (yet)—don't fix it
   - Collapse occurs long after an ecosystem's carrying capacity has been exceeded
   - We don't need to act for the sake of "uncertain" projections about, for example, global warming, ozone depletion, food shortages, etc.
   - If it's not *my* problem, it's not a problem (e.g., social security, starvation)

8. Until scientists can prove a phenomenon beyond scientific doubt, society doesn't need to act on it
   - No one can *prove* that smoking causes lung cancer
   - Risks should be managed by the free market
   - Ecological threats are more like people (innocent until proven guilty) than like drugs (guilty until proven innocent)

9. Innovations (technological and others) can push back biological limits indefinitely
   - Malthus was "wrong" because of the "green revolution"
   - We don't need to worry about unintended, negative consequences of technological "solutions" (i.e., solutions often produce a new and different set of problems). The "next" technological breakthrough will solve the problem
   - Some still think we could ship excess people to another planet

I promised I'd begin with a quick analysis of a killer thought that most readers might find easy to deplore. You probably are unclear as to what the second killer thought in Table 6-1, "The future is to be discounted" actually entails. Economists tell us that each of us has a *subjective discount rate*. Suppose I told you that you've just won one million dollars that I'll pay to you as a lump sum ten years from now. You are happy—unless you heavily discount the future (i.e., you have a high subjective discount rate)—such people might actually have a stronger negative reaction to having to wait ten years to get their money than they react positively to getting the windfall.

Suppose that I offered to blunt your negative reaction to having to wait (i.e., to delay gratification) by offering to give you $900,000 now in lieu of your million dollars one decade from now. Would you take my offer? Most people would jump at the offer, which suggests that they have a subjective discount rate of about *1 percent or higher* (they would take 10 percent less money to get it ten years earlier). Would you take $500,000 now? Many people would. Their subjective discount rate would be about *7 percent or higher.* [If you think you could take the $500,000 and use it to earn enough to have more than a million in ten years, you're probably kidding yourself. The current, highest yielding, safe investment (thirty-year U.S. Treasury Bonds) get 6.5 percent. In ten years $500,000 would grow to $938,569—*if* you didn't pay taxes, but the IRS would not like that at all.]

Our research suggests that subjective discount rates typically run from 5 to 15 percent. Psychologically speaking, higher subjective discount rates suggest our willingness to give up pleasurable events in the future in order to gratify ourselves in the present. People (corporations and countries also) who are in debt have much higher subjective discount rates than do solvent people, corporations, and nations since debtors are more likely to be desperate for money in the present.

About twenty years ago the United States was a net creditor nation. We also had a well-run national retirement trust fund—Social Security Insurance. My parents paid in a small amount each year in order that they might withdraw their money (plus whatever their contributions had earned) during their retirement years. This is the opposite of discounting the future—it is a wonderful case of making a sacrifice in the present to ensure a pleasant future. But we have allowed our politicians to loot the Social Security Trust Fund, and it is now projected to go broke long before the time my generation retires. Thus, people my age probably will get nothing in return for the forty years of contributions we made.

A convenient year to mark the retirement of my parents' generation, and the start of the stewardship of my generation, would be 1975. Similarly, 2015 is a convenient year to designate my generation's retirement, and my children's assumption of responsibility for the payment (through taxes) of our country's collective debts. Thus, we're about half-way through my generation's term of stewardship. What does our financial report card look like thus far? I'm afraid we've all but failed out! We had no national debt to speak of in 1975. Today our collective indebtedness stands at almost $5 trillion! The interest expense we incur, to service that monument to our collective selfishness over the last twenty years, is about $700,000,000 *each day.* Our government either spent too much or collected too little in taxes (or both) over the past two decades. Each of the last twenty unbalanced, yearly budgets that our elected lawmakers approved was an explicit *discounting* of our collective future—and now those chickens are coming home to roost. Those lawmakers (back in 1975) acted as if they could not care less that they were creating colossal problems for the lawmakers of 1995. Why should they have acted differently? After all, how many of the 1975 office-holders are still in office? It's now somebody else's problem. "Eat, drink, and be merry—for tomorrow we die." What the old maxim conveniently ignores is that our "eating, drinking and being merry" might leave our children (and their children also) with financial liabilities (as well as enormous ecological liabilities) that keep our descendants from ever having the opportunity to eat, drink, and be merry.

You'll notice, as I briefly discuss the other eight toxic thoughts in Table 6-1, that there is considerable overlap among the nine toxic thoughts. The toxic beliefs represent interwoven strands cut from the cloth of the maximization/optimization view of human nature. The first killer thought in Table 6-1 is that "Consumption will produce happiness." Because so many people in affluent societies are now engaged in extremely high levels of overconsumption, several writers have observed that this might suggest a crisis of the human spirit (Gore 1992), or an addiction by many members of contemporary societies (Glendenning 1995), or even the madness of modern society (Shepard 1995). While it is true that people in poverty may tend to be unhappy, once a person's basic needs are met, there is *no* relationship between increased consumption and happiness. In fact, from a psychological perspective, increased buying and consumption are often produced by bouts with sadness, emptiness, loneliness, and/or depression, and thus are often symptoms (or an attempted cure) of unhappiness or unmet emotional needs. People need to learn to deal with negative emotional states and with emotional needs. The numbing and distracting that result from buying and consumption can lead to a self-defeating downward spiral. The book *Can't Buy Me Love* by Coleman and Hull-Mast (1992) provides an enlightening discussion of these issues.

Businesses sometimes imply that people will lose their jobs if consumers spend less. While this might be true (in the short run) for people in certain jobs (e.g., advertising, sales clerks), a higher savings rate is generally associated with a good economy rather than an unhealthy economy. Since the United States currently has one of the lowest savings rates among all developed countries, greater savings (and thus less consumption) will in all likelihood lead to more jobs in the long run. Putting the first two toxic thoughts together yields the claim of the third entry that, "Present consumption is preferred to investment in (or conservation for) the future." Madison Avenue churns out billions of dollars worth of advertisements each year designed to convince people that they ought to buy an array of goods and services that they do not need. Chapter 11 deals with this form of consumer brainwashing in greater detail. Also, helpful strategies for using prices to blunt consumer preferences for certain destructive or wasteful products (e.g., "green taxes" as described in Chapter 5) are often resisted by this toxic thought, in spite of the fact that they serve to discourage wasteful, present consumption for the sake of a better future.

The fourth killer thought is that "Growth is good." While I label the belief in growth as a killer thought, it is *not* that growth is always bad, or that the notion of exponential growth is necessarily evil. Rather, Kenneth Boulding, former president of the American Economic Association, stated the form of the toxic thought precisely as, "Only madmen and economists believe in *perpetual* exponential growth" (quoted in Hardin 1993, p. 191). Again, such unquestioned valuing of growth comes from acceptance of a maximization/optimization vision of human nature. Similarly, while B. F. Skinner believed that a person's ultimate goal in life was to maximize pleasures while minimizing punishments, we ought not to subscribe to so myopic a purpose for our lives. Finally, if we see ourselves as slaves to "selfish genes," and thus continue to produce too many offspring, we court catastrophes whose magnitude will dwarf all previous human tragedies. Thoughts of *unlimited* growth that were fine for an underpopulated world can be lethal today.

We frequently credit free market capitalism for producing the unparalleled wealth we see in the United States today. I'd agree that our version of capitalism was quite well suited for the world of the nineteenth and early twentieth century. However, capitalism might have to modify some of its tenets (and excesses) in order for it to be a positive force in the twenty-first century. In particular, the three thoughts under "Free market capitalism is the best system" suggest what we will need to counter in order to develop a type of capitalism that is more helpful for the future. In particular, capitalism must find ways to reduce economic throughput—to keep the magnitude of human impact on the environment to a minimum. Recall the I = PAT formula from Chapter 4. If you insist on having a large human population (P), then the level of affluence (A) must be minimized in order to not overtax ecosystems. Similarly, the CC-PP (communize costs—privatize profits) game (see Hardin 1993, chap. 23) that is currently played by businesses represents their attempt to externalize as many of their costs as possible. For example, paper manufacturers use public streams to dispose of dioxin. The cost of cleaning up the streams fall to all of us (it has been communized). However, the profits from the sale of the paper are privatized (they belong to stockholders and corporate executives). This leads us to the sixth killer thought, "Paying less for something is always better than paying more." This notion runs counter to the wisdom of "Green taxes," which use prices to signal to consumers that certain products involve great destruction to produce (or dispose of) while their competitors do not. The resulting ecologically wise free market will then help consumers to do the right thing (since it will then also be in their financial best-interest to do so).

The seventh toxic thought, "If it ain't broke (yet)—don't fix it," speaks to our lack of belief in the wisdom of the old maxim that,

"An ounce of prevention is worth a pound of cure." Humans have developed remarkable powers of *foresight*. We can now "fore-see" the ways in which many current trends will impact the world in the future. Should we act now (i.e., incur short-term costs) to avoid likely, future disasters (i.e., avoid severe long-term costs)?

By the time my father was forty-seven years old (my current age), he had lost all of his teeth. I now have all my teeth (in large part) because our government put fluoride in our drinking water—my father didn't have the benefit of this foresight when he was young. I can still remember some elected officials being reviled because they were "unwittingly caught-up in a communist plot" (they incurred short-term political costs) as they committed valuable tax dollars to the fluoridation program (short-term monetary costs) to make my physical and financial future better some forty years later. I had my first root canal last week. It's now only a forty-minute surgical procedure, but it cost me $622. Putting a cap on the tooth costs an additional $500. If I hadn't drunk fluoridated water as a child, I might have had much more dental work by now. In a sense, I might now be over ten thousand dollars richer because a small amount of money was invested in preventative efforts (water fluoridation) forty years ago. And those calculations consider only the money-benefits of having healthy teeth. Chapter 8 shows explicitly how a series of small, short-term investments can almost miraculously yield a mountain of long-term benefits—it's just simple arithmetic.

Every projection of a future event must be made with some degree of uncertainty. People with a vested interest in maintaining the status quo often focus upon this inevitable uncertainty in future projections to argue that scarce, current funds should not be "squandered" on an outcome that might not occur. This strategy leads us to the eighth toxic thought, "Until scientists can prove a phenomenon beyond scientific doubt, society doesn't need to act on it." However, philosophers of science know that science never produces certainties. Science yields the most likely truths currently available. Still, every reasonable human being knows that we must sometimes act based upon extremely well grounded (but not absolutely certain) scientific knowledge.

The final killer thought is "Innovations (technological and other) can push back biological limits indefinitely." In 1798 Thomas Malthus published his essay on the principle of population. In it he noted that while population increases geometrically (i.e., exponentially), food production increases arithmetically. Given this discrepancy in growth rates, Malthus predicted that there would soon be severe food shortages and widespread famine. What Malthus didn't know was that humanity would experience a "green revolution"—the most spectacular set of agricultural innovations ever seen. While the rate of human population growth has been even greater than Malthus predicted, the rate of increase of food production over the last two hundred years has been absolutely breathtaking. However, it seems that we might now have reached the end of the green revolution, as worldwide, per capita food production appears to have peaked around 1984 and has declined every year thereafter (see Brown 1994).

Since population continues to grow exponentially, further agricultural breakthroughs are necessary just to keep the current rate of decline in per capita food production from plunging even more steeply. However, the green revolution was *not* produced simply by technological advances (e.g., fertilizers, crop rotation, herbicides, improved tilling practices) that increased per acre crop yields. Throughout the course of the green revolution each year far more new acreage was put into productive service than was lost to soil erosion, salinization from over-watering, pesticide poisoning, and the like. However, all of the easily farmable lands worldwide have already been put into use. New acreage now comes through the burning of tropical rain forests (where the soils are typically suitable for only three to four years of monoculture farming), on steep hillsides (that are highly susceptible to erosion), or in river floodplains (that will inevitably be flooded). Thus this replacement acreage is far more unreliable than the previously productive land that is being lost. More farmland now goes *out* of service each year than can be replaced by new acreage—with no deceleration of this alarming trend in sight.

We must remember that our thoughts are sometimes toxic and sometimes healing. Thus, it is important to periodically examine the effects of our current ways of thinking to determine if their effects will be beneficial in the rapidly changing world of the twenty-first century. For there are few things in life as destructive as an old orthodoxy that has outlived its usefulness. We must constantly examine the content of our thoughts to determine whether they are still life-friendly.

Part II

Act Locally

L OOMING ECOLOGICAL PROBLEMS are global in scope. Thus, it was important to understand them initially from a global perspective, as we did in Part I. However, in the face of any challenge, thought without action is vacuous. Thus we will now consider how each of us might begin the task of changing our thoughts, actions, lifestyles, and institutions so that we are each more a force for a global solution than we are a part of the global ecological problem.

At age forty-two, ecology meant nothing to me. I had fathered only two children (that's good) but lived a typical upper middle–class lifestyle (that's very bad). But I did neither for ecological reasons. I was probably less ecologically aware than most readers of this book, as virtually all of us were less ecologically aware in 1990 than we are now. However, a series of completely unplanned experiences led me to an awareness of current ecological realities. Once aware of the terrible trajectories of many ecological trends, I came to see several of my unexamined beliefs in a new (and troubling) light.

I could no longer see human beings as unqualified "goods;" growth and development could no longer be given the benefit of the doubt as valuable trends; and free market capitalism (as currently practiced) could no longer be seen as beneficial to human life in the long run. These changes in my beliefs occasioned changes in my lifestyle also. However, another way to change one's beliefs is to first change one's actions in the desired direction. Thoughts have a way of following new actions. The goal toward which change must take in our lives is simple to identify. We must incorporate the five principles of sustainability into our patterns of living. How can we take part in programs of conservation, recycling, renewable resource use, restoration, and population control?

Part II represents something of an autobiographical sketch of the journeys I've taken over the past few years. It also depicts how ecological psychology might be practiced, because I am a psychologist who wishes to understand present ecological realities. I employ case studies, single-subject experiments, group experimental investigation, and conceptual analyses to make sense of our problems and to decide what to do about them. Clearly, a chemist, biologist, economist, or political scientist would have approached each of the problems in the subsequent chapters quite differently. Thus, the nature of each problem—and putative solutions in each case—would have been quite different. In fact, I'd be thrilled if someone in each scholarly discipline would do exactly that. Because our problems are multiply caused, multifaceted programs to attack these difficulties stand the greatest chance of prevailing. As Jamesian pluralism so beautifully instructs, the truth about anything we study lies in the areas of agreement among answers that have been approached from a multiplicity of conceptual perspectives (scientific, religious, social, cultural, psychological, humanistic, political, etc.) that we bring to bear on the issue. No single discipline is responsible for our present difficulties, and no single discipline can possibly define a cure for these maladies.

Chapter 7 (The Light Bulb Kid) tells how I was provoked into a course of action to make the dormitories at Notre Dame a bit more energy-efficient (a conservation program). Chapter 8 (Habits at First Are Silken Threads) asks readers to carefully examine their use (and abuse) of money. Is money something to be used and consumed—or is it a resource to be shepherded and conserved? The silken threads of habits of saving, investing, spending, and living beyond our means (i.e., living financially unsustainable lifestyles) are carefully examined in both Chapter 8 and Chapter 10 (Cheap Is Beautiful). Living a financially sustainable lifestyle is a fine way to begin to live an environmentally sustainable lifestyle. Chapter 9 (Recycling Trashy Systems) demonstrates how complex it is to practice the recycling principle of sustainability.

Water is one of the most basic needs in life. Chapter 11 (Water, Water Everywhere: But Is It Safe to Drink?) demonstrates how difficult it is to know the value (e.g., purity, effectiveness) of the many liquids that we ingest. Finally, the Appendices present concrete attempts to conserve energy in my daily life and to encourage others to do likewise.

The examples in Part II mostly consist of local efforts to address local problems. Focus on local issues is almost a necessity when one looks for specific, ecologically important actions to incorporate into one's lifestyle. Thus, if an author from another part of the country had written this book her or his projects and solutions would have been quite different from those found in Part II. The heterogeneity in ways one might work toward a healthier environment becomes staggering when one considers how ecological activism is pursued in other parts of the world. Books such as Savitt and Bottorf's (1995) *Global Development* will supplement the, of necessity, truncated range of projects detailed in Part II.

My hope is that Part II will stimulate each reader to embark upon an ecologically oriented journey of his or her own. Is it surprising that a psychologist would believe that millions of programs of self-change by individual human beings might be an important first step on the road to making needed political, economic, and social changes? If we are successful, sometime in the future our species might once again achieve the status of a "good citizen" of the community of life on earth.

THE LIGHT BULB KID

"IDEAS, VALUES, AND IMAGES" is a required course for all majors in Notre Dame's College of Arts and Letters. This year-long experience is divided into sections on "Nature," "Society," "The Self," and "God." In the section devoted to Nature, students read about some of the current ecological threats to "lifeboat earth" such as famine, overpopulation, desertification, ozone depletion, deforestation, soil erosion, global warming, and water, air, and solid waste pollution (Brown, Flavin, and Postel 1990, 1991). These discussions are always depressing experiences, as our sophomores become ever more aware of the fact that the world they will inherit will be saddled with a number of threats to human life whose terrifying trajectories have greatly accelerated during the time my generation has exercised stewardship of mother earth.

The last discussion on ecology in my fall 1991 course was a particularly depressing one. But a sophomore named Ryan Sweeney tried to interject a note of optimism into our discussion by suggesting, "Instead of just talking about these problems, why don't we try to do something about them." His classmates immediately derided his naiveté. So rough was their attack that I feared for Ryan's mental health. I made it my business to walk across campus with the kid as we left class, and since I possess the union card, I figured I'd try to give the poor fellow a bit of supportive psychotherapy. But Ryan didn't need my support—he was afire! He argued that Notre Dame was inefficient in its use of electricity in the dormitories—and he wanted to do something about it. Since I always urge students to try to convert their values into actions, I suggested that he might contact the University's electrical engineers, purchasing officials, and plant administrators. But I felt guilty about encouraging Ryan to do so, for I was certain that I was throwing yet another Christian to the lions. That a sophomore psychology major might have a better idea about dormitory lighting than a swarm of engineers was, frankly, beyond my ken.

Over the course of the next year, Ryan dutifully reported his litany of deadends to me. "What do you want, kid?" "Cost ineffi- cient!" "Impractical!" "You have no idea of the technical difficul- ties." "Studies demonstrate that our present system is the optimal system." Ryan was not even able to get sufficient information to determine whether his plan might be cost-efficient. Each time he waited outside my office for his turn to see me, Ryan would recount to our departmental secretaries his latest encounter with a brick wall. Finally, one day a secretary asked me, "When are you going to stop torturing that poor light bulb kid?" I knew she was right, so I wrote a testy letter to Father William Beauchamp, Executive Vice President of the University of Notre Dame. I asked him if every- thing in this world *must* be cost-efficient. Was Notre Dame unwill- ing to spend even a penny to honor its ecological values? Beauchamp fired back a reply. Of course Notre Dame would put its money be- hind its ecological values, but the costs needed to be reasonable and the ecological benefits significant to justify the expense. We were instructed to use his technical staff to produce a concrete proposal that did not necessarily need to pay homage to the god of cost- efficiency.

Ryan was thrilled; now he'd learn if his idea was any good. I, on the other hand, was terrified; my boss had told me to put up or shut up. Since I was set to leave the snows of South Bend for spring vacation at Disney World, I instructed Ryan to find out the cost involved in converting to high efficiency bulbs, and to calculate the cost effectiveness of such a move.

"This is great!" Ryan exulted as he hurried out of my office.

"How much do these bulbs cost?" I yelled after him.

"They retail for $24.50," he fired back.

"A dozen?" I queried.

"A bulb!" came the reply.

By the time I was revived, Ryan was gone. I could have sworn I heard my father softly asking, "Boy, what's the use of having a big mouth if you can't put your foot in it about once a day?"

Despite the allures of the Magic Kingdom, I decided to balance my vacation by reading Vice President Al Gore's fascinating book, *Earth in the Balance,* which I'd been asked to review for a psychol-

ogy journal. In the first 300-odd pages, Gore convinced me that
Ryan was prescient in his desire to reduce electrical consumption.
After automobiles, the generation of electricity is considered the
chief contributor to threats such as acid rain and global warming.
But I was still afraid that at $24.50 per light bulb, we would be
asking Notre Dame to dig deep into its pockets. Then two paragraphs in Gore's book hit me like a bolt of lightening:

> The redesign of devices that use energy inside the building can
> also have a dramatic effect. One of the most striking examples is
> the new generation of light bulbs—though they are still not widely
> used—which give the same amount of light as the older generation
> of bulbs while using a fraction of their electricity . . . the wide-
> spread use of these new bulbs could by itself dramatically reduce
> energy consumption throughout the industrial world. The light
> bulbs now in common use are based on a pre–World War I design
> that sends the electrical current through a metal filament made
> mostly of tungsten; the filament glows and emits light, but the
> metal filament produces almost twenty times as much heat as light,
> meaning that most of the electricity is wasted. The new bulbs are
> based on an improved fluorescent design that sends the electrical
> current, not through metal, but through a gas that glows with light
> but loses very little energy in the form of heat. Unlike earlier fluo-
> rescent bulbs, the new ones fit regular sockets and fixtures and offer
> a quality of light every bit as pleasing as that of our incandescent
> bulbs and just as much of it. Yet they last more than ten times
> as long.
>
> One may well ask why they are not being used. The answers are
> instructive. First, there is simple inertia. Consumers are generally
> not aware that the new bulb exists: few stores sell it, wholesale dis-
> tributors don't keep it in stock, and the resulting low demand
> has limited the interest of manufacturers in high-volume produc-
> tion that would bring down the price. Moreover, the government
> provides no leadership whatsoever to encourage the transition. But
> there is something else at work as well: the initial cost of purchas-
> ing each new bulb is about $15, several times greater than that of
> a standard incandescent bulb. Over the lifetime of the bulb, the
> electricity savings far exceeds the total cost of the bulb, but most
> people—and governments—do not calculate costs and benefits
> that far into the future. This is a shame, because a single new
> energy-saving bulb, compared to a standard bulb, *saves a ton of coal*
> over its lifetime. (p. 332)

I screamed "Eureka," kissed Donald Duck, and sincerely wished I were back home in frozen South Bend. Gore had shown me how an expensive compact fluorescent might actually *save* Notre Dame money over the life of the bulb.

In the next two months Ryan conducted cost-effectiveness analyses, solved technical problems with the Notre Dame engineers, and negotiated deals with sales representatives and engineers from the Orsam Bulb Corporation. In all of those meetings no one showed Ryan any disrespect or referred to him as "kid." It was always, "Yes, Mr. Sweeney," and "Thank you, Mr. Sweeney."

Initially, Ryan and his friends replaced about 4,000 incandescent bulbs in campus residence halls with energy-saving fluorescent bulbs. Once the electricity savings had been documented with this initial group of bulbs, we replaced another 4,000 incandescent bulbs in dormitories in fall 1992. Over the next five years, thanks to Ryan's efforts, there will be at least 7,296,000 fewer pounds of carbon dioxide (a greenhouse gas), 28,000 fewer pounds of nitrous oxide (smog), and 52,800 fewer pounds of sulfur dioxide (an acid rain component) in the air that we all breathe. That means lakes in Ohio will be a bit less acidic, forests in New York will be a little less likely to suffocate from pollution, and numerous other ecological benefits will result that a psychologist like me is ill equipped to even imagine. To my mind we are all in Ryan's debt.

Since Ryan refuses to kneel before the totem of cost-efficiency, he will be furious that I am about to reveal the bottom line of his project. From his point of view, the project was worth doing no matter what it cost. But I'll tell you anyway. Over a five-year period, Notre Dame will realize net savings in excess of $190,000. Not bad for a junior.

Ryan is teaching high school and coaching football in California now. As a senior he studied the ecological benefits of promoting the residential use of fluorescent bulbs. Ryan probed the effectiveness of various marketing strategies in promoting residential conversion to energy efficient lighting. That experience was something of a first for me, as I'd never supervised an undergraduate research project that was supported by generous grants from corporations and the Office of the Executive Vice President of Notre Dame. I'd say that Ryan's "naive" work had finally caught people's attention.

More importantly for me, Ryan showed me how persistence in

the service of important goals can sometimes produce real gains. Over the last four years, one idea has led to another, one project suggested yet other endeavors, and each ecological topic led me to a consideration of related problems and topics. The next several chapters can be seen as the results of my personal odyssey—a trip that I never would have undertaken were it not for the inspiration of the light bulb kid.

8

HABITS AT FIRST ARE SILKEN THREADS

A N OLD SPANISH proverb claims that, "Habits at first are silken threads—then they become cables." This chapter will consider small differences in college graduates' habits in saving money. We will see that, in time, silken saving habits can produce cable-like forces that strangle otherwise "successful" careers and lives. Entertain a thought experiment about four successful Notre Dame graduates (two married couples). The force of this exercise will come from its fidelity to the actual financial facts of recent Notre Dame graduates' experiences. The lesson is that small, silken differences in savings habits can, over time, create levels of debt that seriously diminish the quality of our lives. This is because (as the seventeenth-century proverb warns), "If money be not thy servant, it will be thy master."

A Thought Experiment

Imagine two sets of identical twins (one set of males [Adam and Bob], one set of females [Alicia and Barbara]) who decided to marry one another (Adam marries Alicia: Couple A; Bob marries Barbara: Couple B) upon graduating from Notre Dame. My reason for imagining pairs of identical twins who marry is that I want to make these pairs equal in every way (e.g., intellectual prowess, motivation and work habits, investment acumen) save one—Couple A likes to spend 95 percent of their after tax income, while Couple B chooses to spend 85 percent of their after tax income. That one, small difference between the pairs of imaginary couples will be responsible for *all* their differences in assets at retirement. The habit of spending 85 versus 95 percent of income represents a fragile thread that over a forty-three–year working career can create a debt cage.

A few realistic starting values and constants must be determined before we can begin our thought experiment. In my "Psychology of Everyday Life" course I note that Notre Dame Arts and Letters graduates average $26,000 for their starting salaries. If both spouses work, the couple would earn $52,000 per year before taxes. The IRS estimates that such a couple would pay approximately 23 percent for federal, state, local, and social security taxes. This estimate is too low if the wage earners are self-employed, and for the couples' later working years when the incomes are much higher. However, the 23 percent tax bite will be considered constant throughout each couple's working career.

Notre Dame's Office of Financial Aid says that the average level of student loan indebtedness of graduates is now $16,250—or $32,500 for each couple. Students also tend to have about $3,750 ($7,500 per couple) in other debts (e.g., credit card debt, personal loans, auto loans). Thus, the starting value for salaries for Couples A and B in Table 8-1 is $40,000, and the couples' assets are entered for both as a $40,000 debt. The interest rates on student loans range from 5 to 7.4 percent; auto loans are currently around 9 percent; while my colleagues' credit cards charge from 16 to 21 percent annually on unpaid balances. An overall interest rate of 10 percent was chosen for this exercise.

My retirement money has averaged 7.15 percent (TIAA: bonds) and 14.06 percent (CREF: stocks) in annual returns for the last ten years—thus a 10 percent return on investment seems reasonable. If one chooses different starting values and constants, the net wealth of each couple at retirement will change. Later in this chapter other models will be run where different starting values and constants are used, in order to see the results of different scenarios. But since starting values and constants are the same for both the thrifty (B) and spendthrift (A) couples, the *difference* between the assets in Table 8-1 of Couples A and B at retirement represents the results of their different savings habits after forty-three years.

Table 8-1 reveals that Couple A (5 percent savings rate) must immediately declare personal bankruptcy if they retire at age sixty-five, since they are $325,987 in debt and they no longer have salaries that justify carrying such a high level of personal indebtedness. Couple B (15 percent savings rate) retires with a positive net worth of $3,841,246. Since all factors (including professional success as

Table 8-1

Differences over time in assets for a couple who saves 5% of their after tax income (Couple A) versus a couple that saves 15% of their after tax income (Couple B)

| | | Couple A | | | Couple B | |
| | | | Interest | | | Interest | |
	Salaries of A and B	Assets A	Expense A (yr)	Savings A(yr)	Assets B	Expense B (yr)	Savings B (yr)
Start	40,000	–40,000			–40,000		
End yr 1	42,000	–42,000	4,000	2,000	–38,000	4,000	6,000
End yr 2	44,100	–44,100	4,200	2,100	–35,500	3,800	6,300
End yr 3	46,305	–46,305	4,410	2,205	–32,435	3,550	6,615
End yr 4	48,620	–48,620	4,631	2,315	–28,733	3,244	6,946
End yr 5	51,015	–51,015	4,862	2,431	–24,313	2,873	7,293
End yr 10	65,156	–65,156	6,205	3,103	12,032	(248)	9,308
End yr 15	83,157	–83,157	7,920	3,960	84,708	(6,621)	11,880
End yr 20	106,132	–106,132	10,108	5,054	219,804	(18,604)	15,162
End yr 25	135,454	–135,454	12,900	6,450	460,414	(40,097)	19,351
End yr 30	172,878	–172,878	16,465	8,232	877,319	(77,511)	24,697
End yr 35	220,641	–220,641	21,013	10,507	1,586,273	(141,341)	31,820
End yr 40	281,600	–281,600	26,819	13,410	2,775,942	(248,701)	40,229
End yr 43 Age 65	325,987	–325,987	31,046	15,523	3,841,246	(344,971)	46,570

| | $32,598 in interest expenses due every year of retirement without reducing total indebtedness | $384,124 of interest is available every year of retirement without touching principle |

( ) in Interest Expense reflects a positve return on investment. Also, all returns on investments are treated as tax deferred, since 15% of earnings can be tax sheltered each year under combinations of company retirement plans, SEPs, Keoghs, and IRAs.

measured by annual salary) were equal for both couples, the enormous differences in terminal outcomes (bankruptcy versus wealth) are due *solely* to the couples' different saving habits (i.e., 5 versus 15 percent).

Out of the Depths of Debt I Cry unto Thee

When I went to college, most people graduated debt-free. Those of us who couldn't afford the price of full-time college simply worked during the day and attended night school. Or we might, instead, take a year off to earn money to continue our college education. We held an old fashioned belief—that money ought to be earned before it is spent. To dramatize how our current romance with debt serves to imprison our futures, run a model that simply changes the starting value of each couple's Assets from minus $40,000 to 0. Will this change result in a $40,000 gain to each couple's retirement bottom line? Hardly! Couple A's assets at retirement will now be $2,083,616 instead of being $325,987 in debt. The $40,000 debt at graduation cost Couple A $2,409,603 over the forty-three years of this exercise. Couple B now retires with assets of $6,250,848 instead of $3,841,246. The analysis presented in Table 8-1 highlights a personal characteristic (namely, the couples' savings habits) as the critical cause of Couple A's difficulty. Conversely, this last model suggests that debt might be the root of the problem. By examining the results of several models one begins to recognize that many variables are involved in financial success or failure.

I believe that the finest graduation gift a parent might give would be to retire a portion of a graduate's indebtedness. How can Notre Dame work toward lessening the crushing debt load that threatens to diminish our graduates' futures? Providing more scholarship assistance is an obvious answer. As a member of Notre Dame's Faculty Board on Athletics, I have witnessed contributions by the athletic department of more than $25 million over the last four years into the University's unrestricted scholarships fund. By such enlightened policies, the University strives to lower graduates' crushing burden of debt. For public universities the state legislature performs this debt-reducing function. Because state funds cover most of the costs of public universities, tuition at these institutions are about half what they are at private colleges. In a way, the state gives scholarships to anyone who attends public college.

Finally, what can I do to fight the demon of debt and the crippling habit of profligate spending? Like most educators, I can fairly claim, "Gold and silver I have little . . . " However, I do have access to the minds and hearts of many soon-to-be graduates. Perhaps by helping students in my courses to spin the fragile threads of habits of thrift I can help to avert the tragedies represented in Table 8-1 by Couple A.

In Praise of Foresight

Mark Twain once quipped, "I've seen many tragedies in my life: Fortunately most of them never occurred." As always, Twain revealed deep insights into the workings of human nature at which psychologists can only marvel. Foresight represents a person's finest defense against life's tragedies. The philosopher of science, Sir Karl Popper, highlighted the power of imaginative foresight by claiming that humans are lucky—they can die hundreds of times in their imagination, rather than once in reality. I have gone broke hundreds of times in my imagination. Each time this tragedy occurs, I become a little clearer about exactly what I need to do to lessen the chances of this tragedy occurring in reality. Glasses are prosthetic devices that improve our sight; artificial knees and hips aid impaired mobility. Is there any prosthetic device that might improve one's imaginative foresight? One unlikely candidate is the computer. (See Meadows et al. [1992] for a brilliant example of how the computer can clarify our vision of the ecological futures that await us.)

Some students fight off the implications of the data in Table 8-1 by challenging the assumptions and starting values buried in the model that produces such startling and troubling conclusions. For example, some science, business, or engineering majors will undoubtedly note that their average starting salaries will be considerably higher than the $52,000 that a couple of Arts and Letters majors might expect. Computers allow us to fast-forward to this very different possible future in seconds with a few quick keyboard strokes. We simply change the Salaries starting value from $40,000 to $51,000 (i.e., $33,000 × 2 people = $66,000 minus 23 percent for taxes = $51,000).

Surely, students think, $66,000 per year of income will overcome $40,000 in debt, even if the couple is a spendthrift pair who save only 5 percent of their after tax income. Leaving all factors (save Salaries) in Table 8-1 unchanged and rerunning the model reveals that Couple B's retirement nest egg grows from $3,841,246 to $5,560, 229. While Couple A now does not have to declare bankruptcy upon retiring, their nest egg is a paltry $247,008—less than half a year's worth of salary at the time they retired. It seems that even substantial starting salaries (and 5 percent yearly raises) are unable to offset the effects of debt and profligate spending habits.

These surprising findings validate Logan Smith's observation that, "Solvency is entirely a matter of temperament and *not* of income." Do you know the current average saving rate of American families? I'm sad to say that in 1995 it was a paltry 4.2 percent.

Finally, readers might mistakenly conclude that a couple's problems are over if they (like Couple B) simply save 15 percent of after tax salaries. If, for example, a middle income couple has a large initial debt (like $60,000 or $70,000) and if their investments were to average only 4 to 5 percent per year return, then their assets would be insufficient to meet their retirement needs. Thus, good savings habits, while extremely important, do not guarantee savings success. Progress toward debt repayment and securing ample retirement funds must constantly be monitored to foresee the impacts of any changes in salary, interest rates on debt, inflation, rates of return on investments, and the like.

Growth: Arithmetic or Geometric?

In one of my courses, students are given the starting values and constants that will yield the data in Table 8-1. Their first homework assignment is to calculate the yearly values found in the table. Even with the aid of a calculator, it takes almost a day to calculate the values in Table 8-1.

Values obtained for approximately the first ten years generally conform to students' expectations of how savings and debt grow. But eventually the calculated levels of wealth and debt begin to shock these undergraduates. Why is it that so many people are shocked by the enormous wealth and debt that one can accumulate over time? Lend me a paragraph or two of your time and attention to milk your intuition regarding how we often misunderstand growth rates.

Please answer *each* of the three questions below, *before* reading any further. Which of the following choices would you take in each case?

A) A penny that doubled tax deferred every day for a week, or one million dollars?

B) A penny that doubled tax deferred every day for a month, or one million dollars?

C) A penny that doubled tax deferred every day for a year, or one million dollars?

Few people take the doubling penny for a week—as seven time blocks is clearly a short-term proposition. In fact, the doubling penny is worth only $1.28 after seven doubles. Conversely, intuition usually suggests that a penny that doubles 365 times (question C) would be quite valuable indeed. It is question B (an investment that compounds thirty-one times) that seems to produce a split in college students' intuitions (about half take the doubling penny, the other half take the million dollars). At the end of the second week the compounding penny rises in value from $1.28 to $163.84. At the end of the third week the penny is worth $21,611.52, and it grows to $2,782,418.56 by the end of the fourth week. So the doubling penny wins after four weeks. But the typical month is slightly longer than four weeks—it's thirty-one days. Why quibble over a paltry three more compoundings? Because it makes almost a *20 million dollar* difference ($22,259,344.48 versus $2,782,418.56)!

What is wrong with our intuition when many of us select $1,000,000 instead of the $22,000,000 option (the penny that doubles every day for a month)? Psychologically speaking, we mistakenly think we are dealing with an *arithmetic* progression when, in fact, untaxed, compound interest (and debt also) grows *geometrically*. How can our intuitions be deceived so badly?

Do you remember the graph of global population growth in Chapter 2? Figure 8-1, while presenting the same information also clarifies the distinction between future predictions based upon the assumptions of arithmetic versus geometric growth functions. The dotted line is the theoretical function that depicts the data from year 1000 A.D. to year 1800 A.D.—as if these data were the result of an arithmetic function. Early in a geometric function one can easily mistake it for an arithmetic function, as the predictions do not differ greatly from one another. Humans tend to focus almost solely upon short-term impacts, so assuming linearity (or an arithmetic function) still provides pretty good approximations *in the short run* (even though this assumption is incorrect).

The dashed line is the line of best fit (again assuming linearity) for the data from 1000 A.D. to 1995 A.D. The expected global population in the year 2000 (assuming linearity) would be about

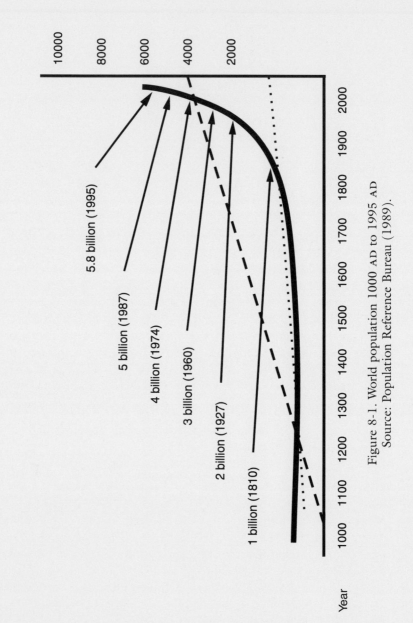

Figure 8-1. World population 1000 AD to 1995 AD
Source: Population Reference Bureau (1989).

four billion people. Given that the earth's population is already close to six billion, that prediction is wrong. Conversely, assuming that population grows geometrically, the data in Figure 8-1 suggest that the planet's population in four years will be about 6.1 billion people. The geometric prediction will undoubtedly prove to be more accurate than the prediction that assumes an arithmetic function (save the occurrence of some worldwide cataclysm—like the death of every human being in North and South America). The point is that over time the predictions of geometric functions differ dramatically from predictions that assume linearity. Thus, late in the games of such geometric functions as compounding debt, untaxed compounding interest, global population, and the like, people are likely to be stunned at how quickly the numbers at stake will increase.

Education for Life

You may not have noticed, but this essay is concerned with building character. It deals with acts of saving and spending, habits of thrift and profligacy, character traits like self-reliance and dependency, and destinies that are financially satisfying or tragic. Rather than being haphazardly related to one another, Charles Reade claims these four domains of human experience are, in fact, hierarchically related:

Sow an act, and you reap a habit.
Sow a habit, and you reap your character.
Sow your character, and you reap a destiny.

The implication of this ordering is that humans should focus upon doing the little things correctly—acts produce habits that build the character that determines one's destiny. A satisfying destiny in life often represents the natural outgrowth of thousands of well-chosen acts.

Education should not remain theoretical and abstract—it should be useful. Education also should help us to lead better lives. For years I have taught students that people overemphasize short-term pleasures and pain relative to any action's long-term consequences in their decision-making calculus. However, I'm afraid such theoretical statements were often far too abstract to exert real impact upon my students' lives. Of late, I have tried to spend more time helping students to trace both the short- and long-term consequences of many actions in their daily lives. Here the computer is rapidly becoming an invaluable resource, and this is not simply true for issues of personal finance. *Sim Earth* is a program that enables students to make choices regarding world population growth in the future, levels of economic activity, amount of investment in ecologically appropriate technologies, and the like. The computer then demonstrates the ways in which our world will change in the future based upon the specific choices the student makes. This complex elaboration of long-term ecological consequences is similar to showing the long-term differences in assets at retirement if one were to select a 5 percent savings rate rather than a 15 percent savings rate. Similarly, *Sim City 2000* enables young public policy analysts to build different constellations of infrastructure (e.g., roads, power plants, schools, libraries) for an imaginary city. The program then spins out a plausible future that favors domains that received investment versus those that are left neglected. My "Psychology of Everyday Life" course also deals with important issues like building and maintaining marital relationships, childrearing strategies, substance abuse, and many more. I am unaware of any *Sim Earth*– or *Sim City 2000*–type computer programs that demonstrate the long-term effects of attention paid to spouses, children, good health, etc. However, I am confident that such aids to our imaginative foresight in these domains will soon become available.

A sound education ought to closely examine the fragile threads of students' habits (such as saving, spending, reading to one's children, serious discussions with a spouse, exercise, etc.) that over time will mold students' characters and create their destinies. For what does it profit our students if they learn about the whole world, but lose control of their own lives?

9

RECYCLING TRASHY SYSTEMS

THE PERSONAL ESSAY has a long and distinguished history as a scholarly endeavor (see Lopate 1995). Unfortunately, the present essay will not represent one of the genre's more glorious moments. It is difficult (perhaps impossible) to craft fresh, dazzling insights into human nature in an essay on garbage. However, unless we take tasteless topics like trash more seriously, the quality of our lives in the future might be badly compromised. My recycling experience serves as a concrete example of how our individual beliefs, values, and decisions interact with local and national systems and policies to determine what each of us will do to address our planet's solid waste problems. In carefully analyzing how my attempts to recycle came about, and then changed in response to a changing local environment, you'll come to appreciate why South Bend and many other American cities are currently recycling wastelands, in spite of the continuing efforts of many citizens to recycle.

My Recycling Story

I need to confess at the outset that for my first ten years in South Bend I did not even attempt to recycle trash. There was a small group of students at Notre Dame ("The Recycling Irish") who maintained a drop-off spot on campus, but I simply didn't avail myself of their services. Each week all of our trash was simply left at the curb in plastic bags on Monday morning and taken away by Superior Waste Systems (SWS). For this service we paid approximately $11 per month throughout the 1980s. I had no knowledge of where the truck took my garbage, or what was done to it upon arrival. I assumed that it was dumped in a huge landfill somewhere nearby which was, in fact, correct.

In fall 1991 SWS, my garbage company, sent letters to all its customers announcing that we could now separate recyclables (e.g., glass, plastic, tin, aluminum, newspapers) from the rest of our trash. We could put them in a large, orange, plastic bin, and SWS would recycle them for us. The cost of this new service ($2 per month) would simply be added to our monthly trash bill.

"Wait just a cotton-picking minute!" I railed. "These jokers expect me to pay $2 a month *extra* for the privilege of doing the right thing? Any lazy slob who continues his or her wasteful ways gets to pay *less* each month than I pay! You don't have to be B. F. Skinner to know that SWS's reinforcement contingencies are all screwed-up."

I thought about calling SWS to tell them their new system would undoubtedly fail unless they charged their extra costs (for new recycling trucks, extra manpower, etc.) to those customers who chose *not* to recycle. But, of course, then everyone would either choose to recycle (to get the lower rate) or switch to one of SWS's competitors who still charged the lower rate for trash removal. Things were beginning to look bad for SWS either way. If they incurred additional costs for initiating a recycling program, they seemed to be putting themselves at a competitive disadvantage to any companies that chose *not* to offer a curbside recycling program. The more I thought about the financing of SWS's recycling program, the more convinced I became that I had no iron-clad solution to the financial problem produced by this new recycling program. Thus, I wisely decided not to call SWS to offer the obvious, gratuitous advice that making customers pay higher rates in order to recycle was producing a system that was doomed to fail.

"Nancy, I'd like to sign up for this new recycling program. It'll only cost us an additional $2 a month to do it."

My wife stared at me quizzically and observed, "It's not like you to want to pay more than you have to for a service."

"I know," I replied, "but imagine how embarrassed I'd be if everyone else on the block recycled and we didn't."

(Paying more than is necessary for a service [such as trash removal] flies in the face of the wisdom offered in Chapter 11, "Cheap Is Beautiful." That is why I identified "paying higher fees to recycle trash" as one of my luxury expenses in that chapter.)

Superior Waste Systems supplied me with a large, orange, plastic bin to hold my recyclable trash. While very few of my neighbors chose to pay more to be able to recycle, a few actually separated out their recyclables and put them into my bin each Monday morning. Clearly their hearts wanted to say "yes" to recycling, but their pocketbooks forced them to say "no." I was a reasonably happy recycler for several years when one day (as unexpectedly as it begun) SWS declared its South Bend recycling program a failure and discontinued the service. The company urged me to keep my orange bin to collect my recyclables and to drop them off at any of the three collection sites in town. As it turned out, the Recycling Irish collection site was about a quarter mile from my office. By this time I was in the habit of recycling (and I now had a recycling bin). Thus, for the last year and a half I have dropped off a bin of recyclables on my way to work one day each week.

Because my SWS trash bill went back to its pre-recycling level, I actually like my present situation better than either of the previous circumstances. While SWS's recycling program was deemed a failure, it was a notable success for me. It got me in the habit of recycling, and then forced me to recycle on my own when their program ended. While I always chafed at having to pay higher trash rates for doing the right thing, I felt too guilty to quit the recycling program because I would have seen this act as subverting SWS's good efforts. But since the company's recycling program is now discontinued, I can save some money while I recycle on my own. From my individual perspective, things couldn't have worked out better.

Superior Waste System's Recycling Story

In order to obtain SWS's perspective on their recycling program, I invited their local vice president to tell me the company's views of what happened to their curbside recycling program. Here is the story he told.

Superior Waste Systems had a small recycling operation in Mishawaka, Indiana that they wanted to expand. At that time, all of their market indicators suggested that there would be a good number of people throughout the county who would participate in curbside recycling programs. Curbside programs are more user-friendly than drop-off programs, especially if the pick-up of recyclables occurs on the same day as regular trash pick-up. In order to keep it user-friendly, a large capital investment was required for new equipment (e.g., recycling trucks) and people to operate the new trucks. Over a period of several years (from fall 1991 to February 1994) participation in the program gradually dwindled to the point where it was economically unfeasible to run five trucks for four days per week over an area as large as St. Joseph County. Peak participation in the curbside recycling program was approximately 5,000 families, and participation had dwindled to about 4,000 families by the program's end. Because SWS is a business—and not a charity—the program had to be discontinued.

However, the curbside recycling program taught SWS some valuable lessons. Prior to the curbside program, SWS had only one level of service, and every customer paid the same amount for full trash removal service. Based upon their curbside recycling experiences, SWS decided to offer a menu of services to customers. For example, one can buy orange plastic bags for $1.88 each, which SWS then collects for free. A 48-gallon toter (garbage can) level of service costs a bit more than the orange bag service, while a 96-gallon toter weekly service level is a bit more expensive still. Unlimited service is $11 per month. Anyone who continues to recycle, I was told, would likely choose one of the restricted service options in order to maximize the monetary benefit of their recycling. Was my face red! I had continued recycling through the Recycling Irish, but had never selected one of the restricted service options. I never knew I had an option—though I am convinced that SWS exerted every effort to advertise their menu of service options. (Before leaving SWS's offices, I changed my service level from unlimited to a 96-gallon toter and I am now saving about $4 per month.)

There was another interesting twist to the SWS curbside recycling program that I learned from our conversation. It turned out that the curbside recycling program would soon be resumed in my neighborhood. How could an economically unfeasible program suddenly become economically viable, due simply to the passage of time?

It turns out that 40 percent of the participation in the county-wide program took place in the town of Granger (where I live). Geographically, Granger covers only 20 percent of the county. Thus, one truck (20 percent of the county-wide program's costs) could collect 40 percent of the program's recyclables. Thus, SWS reasoned, the resumption of only part of the program (in Granger) would be immediately cost-effective. Further, it was risky back in

1991 for SWS to initiate a curbside subscription recycling program because there was no market for the recyclables themselves. However, because of a combination of government initiatives (like mandating that a certain percentage of paper that the government purchased must come from recycled materials) and business initiatives (e.g., constructing mills to reprocess cardboard and newsprint), SWS can now receive payment for some materials that it collects (e.g., cardboard and newsprint) that it had to pay to dispose of in 1991. This combination of factors should make the renewed recycling program profitable immediately.

Finally, the curbside recycling program lowers the volume of waste that SWS must place in landfills. Lowering the volume of materials to be placed in landfills is financially important because gate charges have risen from $7 (in 1991) to $8.60 per compacted cubic yard of trash. This 23 percent increase over four years in this aspect of SWS's cost of doing business is softened by increased recycling efforts. Prior to 1991, SWS collected about 1300 tons/month of recyclables through its public and business drop-recycling contracts. The initiation of the subscription curbside program increased their recyclable load to 1800 tons/month. Surprisingly, total volume did not drop when the subscription curbside program was discontinued. Apparently many other people acted as I did, and continued their recycling efforts through drop-off sites.

But what of the prospects for the resumption of SWS's subscription curbside program? Oddly enough, I'm not terribly optimistic about the renewed program's chances for success.

Approximately 1,600 households in my part of the county were participating in the program when it was terminated. If 1,600 households subscribe for the renewed program, SWS can turn a profit due to reduced costs (one truck instead of five, fewer workers) and income from selling some of the recyclable materials. However the question remains, will people like me resubscribe to the curbside program? Well, if SWS charges me $2 per month for the service, I don't know if I will resubscribe. I can recycle all I want through the Recycling Irish (with Notre Dame paying the cost for pick-up) or through one of several drop sites funded by St. Joseph County. Recycling through a free (to me) drop-off site has become a part of my routine, and I'm not certain I will be quick to pay a price to break a perfectly satisfactory routine. If most of those 1,600 former subscribers react in that manner, then SWS might be surprised to find the "interest in curbside recycling" has cooled in my part of the county. What will I do? I honestly don't know yet.

If the curbside recycling program offered by SWS is free, my decision would be easy. But then the program's costs might not be covered, leaving SWS at a competitive disadvantage to its fourteen local competitors—only six of whom engage in contract recycling, and none of whom have curbside programs. We (as a society) cannot penalize SWS for trying to do the ecologically correct thing. But if the renewed curbside recycling program fails, that is exactly what we will be doing to SWS.

There is a very easy solution to this problem. A well-placed green tax (see Chapter 5) would tilt the competitive balance in favor of companies (like SWS) that encourage their customers to recycle relative to those who do not.

Saint Joseph County's Recycling Story

It seemed natural that I would tell "my recycling story." A high ranking local SWS official seemed the logical candidate to tell "Superior Waste System's recycling story." However, things became complicated as I puzzled over who would be the best narrator of our community's experience with recycling. When I asked others whom they would choose for the task, one name came up more than all others combined. Thus I asked Joe Miller, a professor of psychology at Saint Mary's College who had been instrumental over the years in organizing grassroots initiatives on solid waste problems, to describe St. Joseph County's recycling experience.

The first thing that I learned in the interview with Dr. Miller was that he didn't care to talk much about recycling *per se*. He was interested in outlining a comprehensive, sustainable waste/resource management strategy for the county, which he etched against the larger backdrop of issues of solid waste disposal both locally and nationally. Second, while SWS came off as a hero when they told the story of their recycling program, in Dr. Miller's version of the county's recycling story, SWS comes to be seen more as a cause of the problem than as a frustrated, well-intentioned problem solver. Dr. Miller's vision of the nature of local solid waste problems, and

SWS' role in creating this problem, stands in stark contrast to the view painted by SWS above.

SWS is a wholly owned subsidiary of WMX (formerly Waste Management Inc.) who along with Browning-Ferris are the dominant players nationwide in the solid waste business. In Miller's view, WMX and Browning-Ferris are premier examples of why solid waste disposal is becoming an ever-increasing difficulty nationwide. The problems produced by gigantic, multinational waste disposal corporations lie in three domains: 1) like all businesses, they are profit oriented and their profit comes from disposing of more garbage, not less; 2) their primary allegiance is to their shareholders and the company, not to local residents who must live with the consequences of their actions, and thus they cannot be trusted to do what is in the best interests of people in the local community; and 3) they believe that technological solutions to environmental problems will work in the long run. (Quick quiz—would any killer thoughts from Chapter 6 apply here?)

In St. Joseph County, WMX owns and operates the Prairie View landfill. Originally presented to the county as a small landfill primarily for the county's solid waste, over time WMX has expanded Prairie View's capacity dramatically and the majority of its waste now comes from outside the county.

Briefly, Miller thinks garbage ought to be handled by a local enterprise that operates much like our electric utilities. He envisions a small locally owned landfill that would service St. Joseph's needs primarily. Local control would ensure that the community's long-term safety would not be compromised (through shortsighted, cost-cutting efforts) simply to enhance corporate profits. Trash rates might initially rise to meet the costs necessary to deal *safely* with garbage. This would immediately make programs of source reduction (e.g., using less packaging) and recycling programs much more cost effective. Unlike SWS's program, citizens would not pay to recycle, but would pay more when they did not recycle. Eventually, profits from recycling programs would be used to underwrite the costs of other parts of the comprehensive waste/resource management strategy (e.g., education programs on reusability, repairability, composting of yardwaste, legislative initiatives on source reduction, and legislated use of recyclables). In Miller's words,

St. Joseph County needs a county-owned landfill serving primarily the citizens and industries of this county, with some reciprocity to surrounding counties. Such a landfill should be treated as a resource to be conserved, and should be operated as part of a coordinated comprehensive strategy focusing on waste and toxics reduction, recovery and marketing of recyclables, and procurement of products with recycled content.

A county-owned landfill has numerous advantages over a larger, privately-owned landfill (i.e., Prairie View) that accepts large quantities of out-of-county waste. A county-owned landfill:

- can be kept as small as possible through effective recycling programs, volume based fee schedules, gradually phased-in bans on different types of recyclables, etc.
- be kept as non-toxic as possible by gradually phased-in bans on batteries and household hazardous wastes, reduced acceptance of "special" wastes, etc.
- requires less of our valuable land.
- poses less of a threat to our land values, environment, and roads.
- offers lower disposal fees and longer-term "guaranteed" disposal capacity to residents, business and industry.
- keeps the profits of landfill operations within our community and available for reinvestment.
- avoids burdening our citizens and environment with risks that benefit only distant communities and corporations. (Miller 1993, p. 1).

Given Miller's vision of a sustainable solution to our trash woes, it is not surprising that he would see WMX's business practices as undercutting whatever chances his ideal solution might have of becoming reality. WMX (as many other American businesses) will use aggressive (perhaps predatory) pricing strategies to gain market share. In doing so, they initially lower prices to drive out weak competitors (like our imagined "garbage utility") and then gradually have prices rise to a point where they deliver handsome profits (and/or support temporary, below-cost rates to obtain market share in other markets). Miller's plan involves pricing garbage removal at a level to support locally controlled, excellent strategies for dealing with garbage disposal that will not represent time bombs waiting to explode on later generations. Miller believes that WMX's high-technology, profit-driven business strategies will result in many full landfills that will represent toxic threats to many communities in the not-too-distant future. What evidence does Dr. Miller have for his suspicious view of the actions of WMX and similar companies?

Miller (1993) provides numerous examples of business practices (both locally and in other parts of the country) that give one serious reason to wonder whether such companies *ever* give a community's long-term safety interests any weight in determining their business practices. Miller feels that unless vigilant, local supervision of companies involved in waste disposal (like WMX) is maintained, the community's long-term safety needs will be abused in order to cut disposal costs. This is because it represents an important competitive advantage to any business to have no permanent home—to use and abuse any environment until it becomes unprofitable to do business in that locale. Then this American (or multinational) company simply moves on to another virgin county, state, or country. Here's how Professor Miller made me aware of this reality.

Why does WMX run the Prairie View landfill in south St. Joseph County? They run it because they can turn a profit on the operation. WMX sees itself as locked in a titanic struggle with Browning-Ferris (and other companies) in a survival-of-the-fittest battle to be profitable and survive. That is the situation that free market capitalism is supposed to produce. Any cost reduction (no matter how risky and shortsighted) represents a competitive advantage that WMX owes to itself and to its shareholders to take. If Waste Management doesn't seize this advantage, one of its competitors surely will.

When the Russians retreated before the Germans in 1942, they destroyed their own villages, crops, and transportation systems. They did so in order to deny these resources to their enemy. In 1944, when the Germans were being pushed back toward Germany, they burned the same villages, crops, and transportation infrastructures. No matter which way the war's going, it's hard on the local populace. Please don't try to identify "good guys" and "bad guys" in this tragic, historical episode. That analysis misses the point completely. *War* represents an insane system that robs combatants of whatever rationality, sanity, civility, and morality they might have otherwise possessed. War itself is insanity—as far as human beings are concerned. (It represents an example of a killer thought, as described in Chapter 6.) I've argued that free market capitalism represents another killer thought—as far as the ecology of our planet is concerned. The long-term care that our planet requires always loses out to the competitive advantage that a business can gain by ignoring the long-term, negative consequences of human business activities. Any company that tries to spend a few extra cents to protect the earth's resources automatically gives its competitors another chance to put it out of business. While the CEO of WMX might wish to protect the residents of St. Joseph County by building a landfill operation at Prairie View that *won't* pollute the area's ground water, do the company's employees (and shareholders) wish their jobs (and investments) to be jeopardized in order to protect the health of people in our community? The problem might not be due to bad people, but rather be produced by faulty thoughts. I'd argue that when the long-term health of ecosystems is at issue, free market capitalism no longer represents a healthy system of thoughts. This is because free market beliefs represent absolute belief systems that imagine a world without limits—where more is always better. This type of economic thinking is inevitably lethal to finite ecosystems as soon as the number of humans (and their level of business activity) comes close to the ecosystem's natural capacity to neutralize the waste products caused by this human activity.

Remember we just claimed that the reason WMX is now conducting business in St. Joseph County is because it can turn a profit. The moment it cannot be profitable here, WMX owes it to its stockholders to go elsewhere (e.g., Illinois, Nevada, Mexico, Rwanda) to site its new, low-cost landfills. Because competition is cut-throat in free markets, WMX cannot afford the sentimentality of worrying about how the good citizens of St. Joseph County will deal with their trash problems—or how they will handle the ticking time bombs of old, exhausted landfills.

In Professor Miller's vision of how St. Joseph County might deal with waste/resource management issues, all costs and profits (e.g., from recycling programs) would be used to handle our waste in a sustainable manner in order to avoid future problems. We would pay the *total* cost of our wastefulness now (all externalities would be internalized in the cost calculation of trash disposal)—we would no longer simply dump those externalized costs on future generations. And as St. Joseph County would now deal with its waste, so would other counties also face up to their waste. Currently, over 60 percent of the trash deposited in the Prairie View landfill comes from

sources outside our county. How long can we remain other places'
garbage can? In our current free market version of capitalism, it
seems that few people defend the land's interests. Unless the residents of St. Joseph County are willing to invest in their county's
future, its prospects are grim.

After the Dust (and Garbage) Settles

What might be learned from this welter of complex (often con-
tradictory and counterintuitive) factors implicated in the problem
of solid waste disposal? Several points can be noted easily. First, the
intentions of the people that I interviewed for this chapter are sincerely positive. Each is passionately concerned with the problems of
waste disposal and each is working extremely hard to solve this dilemma—given each person's vision of the cause of the problem. But
therein lies our greatest difficulty. There is no single vision of "the
basic cause of the problem" that all parties can agree upon. At times
the problems look to be caused by the unwillingness of citizens to
pay for their share of the costs of recycling. At other times it appears
to be the laziness or short-term vision of local companies who are
trying to reduce their costs. At still other times, it appears to be a
malignancy that lies at the heart of our free market capitalist system
of doing business. There is a certain amount of truth in each of
these construals of what causes our current solid waste problem, but
no construal gets the whole problem right.

Since there is no single simple cause to the problem, its remedia-
tion will necessitate far more than a single program or policy
change. Many, small, interconnected alterations will be required to
make substantive, permanent changes in the ways we deal with our
garbage. For example, citizens' awareness of the importance of recycling can be improved, taxes on use of virgin resources can be
increased, green taxes on dangerous and toxic wastes can be implemented, business tax incentives for the production of (and purchase
of) materials made from recyclables can be instituted, mandating
the community-directed, local disposal of local waste might be considered, Nobel prize type awards for the best breakthroughs in effectively handling solid wastes could be established, and so forth.
Obviously, not all of these "solutions" will be popular with all parties involved in the solid waste controversy. However, it is clear

that the current system is broken—and thus we must do something to try to fix it. The one point that appears noncontroversial is that present systems are failing us badly—in spite of the well-intentioned efforts of most people involved in the issue. As with most ecological issues, we have too many people living unsustainable lifestyles, serviced by systems that do not enter all the costs of waste disposal in their pricing considerations, and a government (and populace) that is willing to dump the costs of their current profligacy on to an unsuspecting (and unrepresented) generation of our children. It's time we considered recycling this trashy system.

10

CHEAP IS BEAUTIFUL
Is Your Money Working as Hard as You Are?

PERHAPS MY NATURAL frugality comes from my parents' incessant use of maxims such as, "Willful waste makes woeful want," or the simpler, "Waste not—want not." Or perhaps it was their frequent reminders that, "A penny saved is a penny earned." (Actually, a penny saved is equal to about 1.48 pennies earned, if one is in the 31 percent Federal tax bracket, allowing for 14 percent social security taxes, a 3 percent state tax rate, and no county or city taxes—as is the case in South Bend, Indiana.) See what I mean? I'm engrossed with the real, total cost of the things we purchase and consume. It is quite possible that my fixation is due to parental training—or perhaps I was just born to be cheap.

I am amazed at how economically shortsighted are the actions of many intelligent people. For example, most people today are under great economic pressure. Since we all would like to be responsible in our personal finances, my neighbors, students, and friends who find themselves in an economic mess invariably reach for the same solution—*they try to earn more money*. While the impulse might be laudable, I'd like to criticize the wisdom of this strategy. My first objection to the "earning one's way out of debt" strategy is simple. As shown above, it can require $1,480 in additional earnings to achieve the same effect as a $1,000 reduction in spending. (Actually, for me to buy a $1,000 wristwatch would require $1,554 in additional earnings. This is because in South Bend we pay a 5 percent sales tax, and one must also pay federal, state, and social security taxes on the sales tax that we are routinely charged. This wasn't always the case, as we were able to deduct sales taxes paid on our Federal tax return until that rule was changed in the 1980s. But I digress—or do I?)

Rule #1: Spending cuts are far more effective than increased earnings in escaping a household financial crisis. But this fact does not represent my primary reason for bashing the "earn your way out of economic difficulties" strategy. I see terrible, unintended consequences on personal, family, and work productivity and satisfaction when my neighbors take on a second job; when faculty colleagues do more private consulting; when my students get part-time jobs; and so forth. In a real sense, we diminish our lives whenever we overwork. Unfortunately, too many of us are already working too hard—and still we are experiencing financial difficulties. I remember being told about someone who interviewed dozens of dying people and asked how they would live their lives differently, if they were given the chance. *None* said that they would spend more time at work.

As a psychologist, I'm compelled to ask why so many of us are overworking ourselves into early graves, when there often is a more effective solution readily available to ease financial strains? Why don't we recognize the enormous power of spending less, consuming less, and of generally appreciating the beauty of frugality? My opponent in this essay is the cumulative effect of trillions of dollars of advertising propaganda that have been hurled at each of us over the years. My tasks are: 1) to plead with you to seriously reconsider what items in your lives are luxuries rather than necessities; and 2) to show how we might obtain these necessities and luxuries in ways that greatly reduce the amount we spend for them.

I offer these suggestions to help relieve the psychological strain many experience due to financial difficulties. We might thereby avoid the consequences of overwork that result from our efforts to earn our way out of financial messes. As examples, I'll consider the purchase of a range of goods and services—light, diamonds, heat, wristwatches, tuna fish, a housekeeper, and automobiles. I'd love to consider life insurance, but the industry has made that commodity so complex that the analysis would surely exhaust your patience. Finally, thoughts of "cutting back" and "reducing one's standard of living" generally bring about a tightening of the stomach and jaw muscles. Please put away your grim countenance as what I am about to show you is absolutely fascinating.

Are you now under stress due to a lack of money? People with incomes ranging from $5,000 to $500,000 answer "yes" to such queries. But that raises a puzzling question. How can people who earn *100 times* what others earn still have the same problem? The puzzle's solution lies in a reality that comes close to being a universal law of human nature. That is, unless one consciously struggles against the tendency to overspend, one's "necessary expenses" will always grow to equal one's income. So let's first carefully examine some "necessary expenses."

Necessities or Luxuries?

Consider light, a car, a wristwatch, tuna fish, diamonds, heat, and a housekeeper. With the exception of diamonds, I can make a case that all represent necessities for certain people. But the important issue is: Are they necessities or luxuries for me and for you? For me, light, a car, tuna fish (or some nutritious food to replace it), and heat might be seen as necessities—the rest are luxuries. One's circumstances determine what constitutes a luxury. For example, for some of my friends in Manhattan, automobiles are not a necessity. However, in South Bend, Indiana, cars are close to necessary. Since virtually every adult owns a wristwatch, have I erred in calling it a luxury? Not at all. I've never owned a wristwatch, and I can't remember the last time I missed having one. The important point is that something is not a necessity simply because you've always owned one (e.g., a car), or because everyone you know owns one (e.g., a wristwatch). If your life would be significantly diminished by not spending money on an item or service, then it can reasonably be considered a necessity for you. Luxuries are fair game for spending cuts, but unless your financial circumstances are truly desperate, one should not consider foregoing a necessity.

By now, the cynical reader has me pegged as one of those lifeless, grinch-types who wants to suck all the pleasure out of life by making people forego the luxuries that bring joy to life. Rather I'm trying to show ways that enable you to afford even more pleasurable luxuries in your life. What follows is a strategy for maximizing (in the long run) the luxuries that you enjoy. In fact, if you are in the early part of your earning career, and if you can now afford to save 10 percent of your income (using George Clason's [1923] rule of thumb), then no spending cuts are necessary. If you are farther along in your earning career—and are still just making ends meet— a greater than 10 percent surplus is desired. Imagine you cut back on some luxuries, and you now have a bit more money at hand. What should you do with it—stuff it under your mattress?

To What Uses Might Money Saved from Earnings and Spending Cuts Be Put?

What follows is a rank-ordering of good uses for your savings.

1) Pay off debts. When someone turns over his or her personal finances to a pro, this is one of their first moves. Credit card debt gets paid first, prepayment of a home mortgage occurs last.

2) Invest savings where doing so results in income reduction for tax purposes (e.g., SEPs, Keoghs, Company retirement plans) and/ or tax deferred earnings growth (e.g., IRAs).

3) Invest in technologies that produce their own spending reductions. More on this strategy later under "Necessity: Where Is Thy Sting?"

4) Make other investments which result in no particular spending reductions or tax advantage (e.g., stocks, bonds). The importance of this suggestion will increase in the future if a capital gains tax is passed.

The older I get, the more I realize that wisdom is cloaked in simplicity—not complexity. Consider the four suggested ways to use our savings. Why does debt reduction come first? Because interest on our debt represents an expense for which we have nothing to show. Spend money on tuna and you've got something to eat—even with diamonds you at least have something attractive to wear or sell later. The simple wisdom behind the second investment suggestion—tax-favored investments—should have been learned from the "doubling penny" exercise in the last chapter. After thirty-one untaxed compoundings (i.e., doublings) an investment of one single penny grew to $22,259,344.48.

Thirty-one *tax deferred* compoundings is an interesting figure because if you started working (and saving for your retirement) at age twenty-five, your nest-egg would have compounded thirty-one times by age fifty-six. (Of course, our doubling penny example involved two important simplification strategies. Your total contribution to this retirement plan is $.01 [which is ridiculously low] and your annual rate of return is 100 percent [which is ridiculously high].) A more realistic example of the miracle of untaxed, compound interest would be if you invested $2,000 in your IRA account at age twenty-five and received an 8 percent return (the yield on thirty-year U.S. Treasury Bonds as I write). That initial $2000 alone will have grown to $32,000 if you retired at age sixty-one. When that figure is added to the yields from other annual $2,000 contributions you're soon talking about a nice nest egg (approximately $612,000).

Did I say earlier that a 100 percent per year rate of return is ridiculously high? In showing the simple wisdom in suggestion #3 above (i.e., investments that result in future spending reductions), we'll find that 100 percent isn't ridiculous at all.

Necessity: Where Is Thy Sting?

Let's quickly review where we are. For a lucky few, your earnings exceed all your expenses by 10 percent or more—simply invest this surplus in some mix of the four investment strategies above. For many other readers, a number of expenses will have to be identified as luxuries and cut back until income exceeds total expenses by at least the 10 percent per year to be invested. For each of us, surprise items (like a wristwatch) can be added to the usual list of luxury suspects (e.g., movies, vacations, diamonds, lottery tickets, etc.). However, let's consider a more difficult case. For a few readers, even after their luxury expenses have been reasonably purged, their income still might not exceed their expenses for necessities by 10 percent. The key here is to take whatever money you have (no matter how small) and use it to purchase necessities in a way that will cut future expenses.

A story is told that someone asked the economist John Kenneth Galbraith what was the best investment he could imagine. If the questioner had stocks like Thunderbolt Technologies and Wildcat Oil in mind, he or she would surely have been shocked when Galbraith reportedly advised that the next time tuna fish went on sale, he or she was to buy several cans and put it under the bed until it was needed. Let's carefully examine the wisdom in Galbraith's investment strategy. First, we must be dealing with a *necessity*. We know that tomorrow, next week, or next month we'll need tuna fish (or some other nutritious food). Second, the commodity purchased must be nonperishable (buying a hundred loaves of bread that soon mold is ill advised). Third, at my supermarket, tuna normally sells for $.59 for a six ounce can, but periodically goes on sale for $.39. My family consumes about five cans of tuna each week. Thus, if I buy ten cans of tuna on sale, I will save $2.00 in spending over the next two weeks (10 cans at $.59 = $5.90 minus $3.90 (sale cost) = $2.00 savings). A $2.00 savings on a $3.90 investment yields over 50 percent return on investment over a two-week period. One's annualized rate of return would be over 2,600 percent by repeatedly employing this investment strategy. Galbraith is a genius! Further, anyone can come up with $3.90 to begin cutting his or her future expenses. But there are a few minor problems on the horizon for this simple strategy. One must take the $2.00 savings and immediately reinvest it to achieve other expense reductions. (Buy two lottery tickets and you've wasted Galbraith's wisdom.) But there are limits to how much tuna one ought to consume—and it seems that tuna rarely goes on sale just when we need it. Fortunately, savings from wise food investments can be used to lower the future costs of other necessities.

What will you do the next time a 100 watt incandescent light bulb burns out in your kitchen? Try investing your "tuna savings" in a GE 28 watt compact fluorescent light bulb (that sells for $20) that gives comparable light to a 100 watt incandescent bulb (that sells for $.75). "What?" you rage, "Throw away my hard-earned 'tuna money' by overpaying for some high tech light bulb? I thought you said *cheap* is beautiful?" But by now you realize that we're not talking about being "cheap" in this chapter—we're discussing being thrifty, frugal, and financially wise.

Consumers typically look for "bargains," which often turn out to be unwise investments. Investors, on the other hand, are not focused solely upon prices—they consider the likely *rates of return* on their investments. Let's examine the total cost of that 28 watt compact fluorescent bulb versus the $.75 bargain, as we did for the 25 watt compact fluorescent bulb in Chapter 5. First, the compact fluorescent bulb lasts for 10,000 hours versus 1,000 hours for the 100 watt incandescent—so you'll need to purchase ten incandescent bulbs before the compact fluorescent bulb burns out. Thus, the materials costs are $20 for the compact fluorescent bulb versus $7.50 (10 × $.75) for the incandescents. But what of the electricity costs?

If your electricity sells for $.08 per kilowatt hour (the national average) the compact fluorescent consumes $22.40 in electricity over 10,000 hours; the incandescent bulbs consume $80 in electricity. Thus, by wisely investing $20 in a high tech lighting appliance, one saves $45.10 [($7.50 + $80) – ($20 + $22.40) = $45.10].

If your kitchen light is on for about seven hours a day, your electricity savings is realized over four years for an annualized rate of return of over 57 percent per annum. I install a few more compact fluorescent bulbs in my home whenever I have a little extra cash from "tuna money," "cranberry juice money," "toilet paper money," etc. I now have forty (six more than when I wrote Chapter 5) of these lighting money-savers working hard to cut my monthly electricity bill. I've also reduced my heating and air conditioning costs dramatically by installing a geothermal heating and cooling unit when my gas furnace conked out three years ago. The additional cost of the geothermal unit ($3,000 minus a utility company rebate and property tax refunds) is now completely recovered, and the geothermal unit saves about $100 per month in natural gas charges in winter months, and about $50 per month in electricity charges during summer months. As you know by now, money invested in reducing energy consumption also has the positive effect of helping the ecology of our planet, but for the present chapter we'll focus solely upon the economic benefits of energy efficient technologies.

As a final thought on strategy #3, techniques for reducing the costs of necessities, let me tell you that I haven't yet paid $10,000 or more for an automobile. Here's how we do it—we buy used cars from rental companies, rather than autos from new or used car lots. The value of an automobile declines precipitously in its first year of use. The trick is to get a good automobile (rather than picking up someone else's "lemon") after that steep decline in value has occurred. Car rental companies (e.g., Hertz, Avis, National) hold their stock until preset limits (e.g., one year, 30,000 miles) are hit. Or if new stock arrives, some autos are sold before the limits are reached. My last three cars averaged eight months and 22,000 miles of use. Equivalent new autos still on sale (my purchases occurred near the end of the model year) listed for about $8,000 more than the price that I paid. Since rental car companies must turn over all of their stock within a brief time period, the base rate of "lemons" that rental companies sell should be about equal to the base rate of "lemons" sold as new cars—likely a smaller rate of "lemons" than one might find among year-old cars on a used car lot.

In keeping with suggestion #1 to pay off debts immediately, I try to stay with my old car until I have saved enough cash to pay for a "new" car (thus never paying auto loan finance charges). I was able to pay cash for my geothermal unit because one of my used rental auto purchases cost far less than I had expected. My phantom, monthly "car savings," "electricity bill savings," and "natural gas savings" are now used to make prepayments on my home mortgage principal. These additional payments are simply added to the base mortgage payments suggested by our bank each month. Of course, it has taken twenty years of spending frugally to achieve the positive cash flow that allows mortgage prepayments. We might have reached that point sooner had we not chosen (over the years) to purchase certain luxuries. We have always paid top-dollar for childcare and education, we take frequent, short vacations, we receive help with our housework once a week, we make regular charitable contributions, and we contribute to the support of several of our relatives. We were not in a position to enjoy any of these luxuries twenty years ago. However, we trust we will be able to enjoy many more luxuries twenty years from now.

A Psychology for the Twenty-First Century

For centuries, blackness had been seared into our psyches as something ugly, sinister, and loathsome. The black movement of the 1960s began a reprogramming of our collective consciousness with the slogan, "Black is beautiful!" A similar rethinking of the foundations of economic theory, given the coming ecological realities of the twenty-first century, was begun by the British economist E. F. Schumacher (1973) under the title *Small Is Beautiful*. Again, I refer you to the works of Garrett Hardin (1993; *Living within Limits*), Donella Meadows and colleagues (1992; *Beyond the Limits*), and Alan Durning (1992; *How Much Is Enough?*) who will argue against the beliefs that growth and increased consumption represent economic values. We now understand that *sustainable development* (rather than unlimited growth) represent the good to be desired, given the realities of the twenty-first century's overcrowded world.

For too long our thinking has been trapped by the assumptions of "cowboy economics" (see Boulding 1966)—the belief that growth, development, and consumption could go on forever. If something represented a "good" (such as the GDP, the size of a country's population, the amount of luxuries one consumed, etc.), then it followed (from cowboy economics) that more was necessarily better.

The psychology and economics of the twenty-first century will value a *sustainable balancing* of relative goods in our life-choices. Thus, while the consumption of certain quantities of necessities is inevitable, the overconsumption of necessities and luxuries is to be discouraged. Thrift, frugality, and the ability to delay gratification will be cardinal virtues of our psychologies and economics of the future. However, to understand the forces against which these new ways of thinking now struggle, we might consider how advertising strives to convince us that a diamond ring is a necessity.

In a sense, diamond jewelry might be the ultimate luxury. Jewelry is certainly not necessary for life; one can obtain virtually indistinguishable jewelry (using zirconium) for a tiny fraction of the cost of diamond jewelry; and while raw diamonds might occasionally be a good investment, diamond jewelry almost never is. No one in our family has diamond jewelry! But rather than saying that last sentence proudly, I felt *guilty* in acknowledging that fact. Didn't my wife *deserve* a diamond engagement ring? Of course we had a case of graduate students' poverty when we married. But shouldn't I have made up for that oversight with a twentieth anniversary diamond pendant? If my choice to *not* purchase Nancy diamond jewelry simply reflects prudent fiscal management, why would I feel guilty? Pay special attention to the many advertisements for diamond jewelry that you encounter each day. "A diamond is forever!" (Am I less than fully committed to this relationship?); "Buy her a diamond ring, because she deserves the very best!" (Am I indirectly saying to Nancy that she's second-rate?); "A diamond anniversary pin to let her know you'd gladly do it all over again" (Am I having second thoughts about my marriage?). Just because one is a psychologist doesn't mean he or she is immune to psychological persuasion. Am I being frugal? Or am I cheap, uncommitted, unappreciative, etc.? Is it in *anyone*'s best interest for me to be conflicted about my choice to not purchase diamond jewelry?

Frontline did a PBS show on DeBeers—the worldwide diamond

cartel—that showed how control over the diamond trade is maintained by incorporating into the cartel all new sources of diamonds that are discovered. Then DeBeers is faced with the problem of offsetting this additional supply by increasing the demand for diamonds. This is accomplished via a collusion between DeBeers and their retailers that leads to the advertisements quoted above. *Frontline* (1994) provides a blatant example of how these co-conspirators strive to make what is clearly a luxury into a (psychological) necessity. DeBeers laid out its game plan to retailers explaining that a marketing blitz would make the twenty-fifth anniversary pendant *as obligatory as* the diamond engagement ring and the five-, ten-, and twenty-year gifts of diamond jewelry. Of course, DeBeers is reluctant to admit to us that they strive to persuade us that their luxury item is a necessity—they only communicate that reality to their business partners. Nevertheless, a lot of money has been spent (by DeBeers and others) to make me feel guilty about my decision *not* to buy their luxury commodities.

Suppose I were now to decide to buy an anniversary diamond pendent for my wife. One might reasonably ask, "Who has control of my mind? Me or DeBeers?"

This chapter is *not* an anti-luxury diatribe. Rather, it offers strategies for securing the financial ability to enjoy many luxuries over one's lifetime. To the extent that children today are taught to value immediate gratification at the expense of their long-term financial health, it is an essay against this idol of our times. However, some psychologists believe the fight against such idols faces stiff competition.

> [T]he capitalist system, in order to sell its plethora of manufactured goods, has had to enlist the help of the motivation researcher and the Madison Avenue ad agency to get rid of the excessive and ever growing pile of manufactured goods not really needed in our society. To encourage consumption in the absence of real need and to associate status and self-esteem with wasteful consumption, it has been necessary to encourage relatively mindless impulse buying and self-gratification. By now, we have raised several generations of people on endless and repetitive exhortations that it is all right to yield to impulse, to buy without guilt, and to consume without shame. Installment buying may have been the fatal blow to the self-denial of the Protestant ethic. (Albee 1977, p. 150)

None of the wisdom contained in this essay represents an original insight of mine. For example, these ideas merely represent updates and elaborations of the first two (of seven) points for creating personal wealth articulated by George Clawson in 1923, and represent insights originally formulated by Benjamin Franklin in the eighteenth century. (See Robbins [1989] for explicit details on implementing Franklin's wisdom.)

Thoughts on the World's Largest Debtor

Lessons learned in the arena of personal finance may or may not be applicable for remedying the financial ills of a country. However parallels between personal financial strategies and current governmental policies are striking. Consideration of our government's current financial status suggests that some form of fiscal reform is desperately needed. Recall from Chapter 6 that my parents' working careers spanned roughly the forty-year period from 1935–1975. My working career will cover roughly the 1975–2015 period. My children's peak earning years will likely begin in the second decade of the next century. What was the long-term, financial condition of our country as my parents ceded responsibility for paying our country's shared bills in 1975? What will the nation's long-term financial health be like in 2015 when my children take over?

Remember that in 1975 the United States was a net creditor nation, and that we're now almost $5 trillion in debt. The report card at the midpoint of my working-life merits a clear failing grade. For the last twenty years our government has been an anemic earner (e.g., taxes paid) and a profligate spender (e.g., defense, entitlements, interest on debt) relative to other industrialized nations. Most of us have been unknowing participants in a terrible form of financial child abuse. Happily, I still have twenty more earning years to try to improve my final grade. Believe it or not, I am now urging my political representatives to raise our taxes slightly and to cut governmental spending dramatically. (In accord with the earlier finding that spending less is more effective than earning more.) Collectively we need to live more cheaply to ensure that our children are not overburdened by a crushing national debt.

Get that grim look off your face, friend. One of the best kept secrets of our age is that making sacrifices to earn a better future is one of the most satisfying activities that one can undertake. We have been so brainwashed by a culture of consumption and a creed of hedonism that we have forgotten the pleasures that naturally come from building, creating, sacrificing, and conserving (see Albee 1977). The challenge of developing fiscally responsible lifestyles is not a grim sentence to a lifetime of hard labor. Rather, being responsible to ourselves, our children, and their children represents an intriguing challenge, the solution to which will be numbered among our lives' most important contributions. Leaving this world a better place than the world we inherited represents an exciting challenge. How we deal with such important challenges helps to give meaning and excitement to our lives. The winners of the game of life will not be the ones who have consumed the most (and run up the largest debts) when death comes calling—it will be those who gave more than they consumed. While most of us do not evaluate the success of our lives by our wealth, money is an important factor in how successful we are in achieving our lives' goals. This is because (as the seventeenth-century proverb warns), "If money be not thy servant, it will be thy master." If you don't master money, it will conquer you.

11

WATER, WATER EVERYWHERE
But Is It Safe to Drink?

BECAUSE I WAS making good progress in writing Chapter 5 of this book, I was annoyed when my phone rang.

"Hello."

"Professor Howard? This is Tim McNulty." (A pseudonym)

"Hi, Tim. What's up?"

"I called to tell you about this really great job that I got. I'm working with a company that sells these super products that are really great for people and for the environment."

"No kidding, Tim. Can you come over to school to talk to me about the products?"

"That's what I get paid to do. You know, the water around here can be really bad."

Little did I know that Tim's phone call would start me on an excursion that would get me more deeply than I'd imagined into the problem of liquids that we ingest. As an undergraduate who worked on the compact fluorescent light bulb projects, Tim was well aware of my interest in problems of ecology and my commitment to research.

My conversation with Tim a few days later was both exciting and unsettling. It was exciting because Tim finally had a job about which he cared deeply. He looked and sounded great, and he had some products that seemed to hold promise of being good for people and for the environment. However, the conversation was a bit unsettling to me because Tim sounded like a salesman—which happened to be exactly what he was! Like many professors, I had assumed that Tim had thoroughly learned the skeptical, scientific attitude that I thought I was modeling for students in all my classes. Instead, Tim believed in his products—hook, line, and sinker. I wasn't interested in his personal testimonials to his wonderful products—I wanted the facts, the results of dispassionate experiments to demonstrate the value of the products. To my dismay, Tim had no interest in evaluating the effectiveness of his products. Tim wanted me to buy his wares.

I had long been mildly concerned with the safety of my drinking water at home. Our water comes from a well drilled into our groundwater and is not purified in any way. In fact I hadn't had my home's water tested for contaminants in the fifteen years we lived there. You see, I'd been kind of busy, and the water tasted fine so . . . On the other hand, faculty, staff, and students constantly complain about the drinking water in Haggar Hall, which houses Notre Dame's department of psychology. So I plunked down $200 of my money to purchase Tim's filter and decided I was going to determine not only whether our water was safe, but also whether Tim's water purifier was worth its high price.

Tim also wanted me to try a bottle of "Source of Life" (also a pseudonym) which he said was a liquid mineral complex that had miraculously transformed him from the lethargic, generation X'er that I'd known, into the dynamic, upbeat, budding capitalist that I saw before me. I mentioned that nobody becomes a millionaire by becoming a teacher, and that the $200 of mine that he already had was my limit. Being a confident, young capitalist, Tim offered a bottle of this elixir to my research assistant. At the end of this chapter, you can decide whether you think Tim has a promising career ahead as a businessman.

How Pure Is Thy Water?

In this day and age it should be simplicity itself to answer the question in this section's heading. Turns out, it's not—unless you are very rich. My initial design for this study was to obtain two water samples from my home, two samples from Haggar Hall, and two samples from our local, city water supply. One sample from each source would be without the benefit of having been run through my new, countertop purification system. The other sample from each location would have been filtered. A quick review of the literature on water pollutants in the United States revealed that I ought to test for the presence of bacteria, ph, lead, iron, copper, pesticides, herbicides, magnesium, manganese, heavy metals, organics,

Table 11-1
Results of Water Tests

	My home		Notre Dame		City Water	
	Unfiltered	Filtered	Unfiltered	Filtered	Unfiltered	Filtered
Alkalinity*	300	340	360	320	300	300
Chlorine*	<.5	<.5	<.5	<.5	<.5	<.5
Hardness**	1	17	12	21	21	21
Iron*	.1	0	.2	0	.2	0
Ph***	6.9	7.0	7.0	8.0	7.4	8.0
Magnesium**	0	5	5	4	5	8
Manganese*	.03	0	.125	0	.15	0
Calcium**	1	12	7	17	16	13
Copper*	.05	0	.05	.0	.20	.0

* = mg./l.   ** = grains/gal.   *** = idiosyncratic scale

chlorine, chloride, hardness, and dioxin. Notre Dame's Office of Risk Management said that the Environmental Health Lab was the one they used for testing water. A quick call to this lab revealed that they didn't test for bacteria levels. That would need to be done by the County Health Board. However, they would be happy to test for the other contaminants for $5,000 and change *per sample*. Since the balance in my checking account was closer to $100 than it was to the $30,000 price tag for six samples, we will have to be satisfied with a less than complete analysis of our water.

Then how does one go about determining whether one's water is fair or foul? Well, first we tested for bacteria and the samples came out fine. The County Health Board gives no quantitative results, they simply stated that there was no evidence of bacterial contamination. We purchased a Hach water-testing kit for $259 and tested the six water samples. Table 11-1 presents the results of tests on each of our six samples for nine potentially undesirable characteristics.

True to Tim's sales pitch, there were lots of things in our unfiltered drinking water at home, at Notre Dame (from Haggar Hall), and in the city's water system. Of course, in no instance were the levels of minerals for which we tested high enough to constitute a health hazard. Ideally, however, drinking water would contain low levels of these minerals so as not to effect its taste. Meaningful results were obtained on all dimensions except chloride, where changes due to filtration (if they occurred at all) took place in a range lower than our test measured.

Comparison of the filtered and unfiltered columns in Table 11-1 suggests that Tim's water filter was effective in removing some of the minerals (e.g., iron, manganese, copper). If it is important for you to drink water that is free of these minerals, you might want to purchase a water purifier. While a bit overstated, there might be some truth in Tim's sales pitch that, "you can either buy a filter, or be a filter." However, levels of some other minerals (e.g., calcium, magnesium) sometimes actually increased through the filtration process. This is because filtration sometimes works through a process of replacement rather than simple removal. For example, water softeners replace some metals with salt rather than simply removing the metals. To some extent Table 11-1 shows a similar pattern where the levels of some minerals are increased during filtration in order to lower levels of other minerals.

We also decided to conduct some quick studies to see if people could detect by taste the presence or absence of impurities in the six water samples. Twenty-nine people were asked to taste the filtered and unfiltered Haggar Hall water samples and rate each sample's taste independently on a scale from "1" (terrible tasting water) to "10" (great tasting water). The average rating of unfiltered Haggar Hall water was 4.97 while the filtered water was rated 6.28. Thus, the filtered water was seen as significantly better tasting ($t(28) = 2.83$, $p < .01$) than the unfiltered water in Haggar Hall.

There is a more powerful methodological test of differences called linked raters' judgments (Howard and Maxwell 1983; Howard, Obledo, Cole, and Maxwell 1983). In this procedure, judges taste both water samples and then decide which sample tastes better. A rating of their confidence in this judgment is then made on a scale from "1" (can't tell any difference, a guess) to "10" (I'm positive this sample tastes better). Since the filtered water tasted better by the less sensitive technique (reported above), this linked judgment technique was unnecessary in this case. However, if one wants to claim there is *no* difference in taste between samples, then it is critical that the more sensitive and powerful linked judgment technique be used. As expected the filtered Haggar water was correctly rated as the more tasteful sample significantly more confidently ($t(28) = 2.39$, $p < .05$) than the unfiltered sample of water. This difference in taste was likely due to the higher levels of iron, magnesium, manganese, and copper in the unfiltered water sample obtained in Notre Dame's Haggar Hall (see Table 11-1).

A different group of thirty-three people tasted filtered and unfiltered well-water from my home. The two samples were rated as equally tasteful ($t(32) = .33$, $p = 74$) whether filtered (Mean = 6.09) or unfiltered (Mean = 5.91) by the traditional judgment approach. Similarly, there was no reliable preference for either sample ($t(32) = .22$, $p = .82$) using the linked judgment technique. Inspection of the means in Table 11-1 for water from my home reveals very low levels of most elements in the unfiltered samples. Oddly enough, Tim's filter actually *increased* the levels of some minerals (e.g., calcium, magnesium) as part of the filtration process. Thus, we can see that even a filter, which does some good things (e.g., reduces iron, manganese, copper), also produces some unintended negative consequences.

Finally, the two samples of South Bend municipal water (one filtered, one unfiltered) were rated for taste by twenty-seven subjects. The filtered water was judged of equal taste (Mean = 6.07) to the unfiltered water (Mean = 6.18) by the traditional rating techniques ($t(26) = .29$, $p = .77$). Similarly, the linked judgment method found neither the filtered sample nor the unfiltered municipal water sample more tasteful ($t(26) = .27$, $p = .79$).

Given that Tim's water filter worked reasonably well, I began to wonder "perhaps this 'Source of Life' mineral supplement might be valuable also."

You Are What You Eat . . . and Drink

Tim swore that the "Source of Life" mineral supplement had made him a new man. How could a mineral supplement possibly achieve such remarkable results? And if it is effective, why ought we to consider this an ecological issue? We'll let the product's own advertising material describe how it might work, and why the product might speak to larger ecological issues. The advertising claimed:

> In today's fast paced society, our bodies and minds are subjected to a countless array of contaminants, pollutants, pesticides, artificial flavorings and dyes, preservatives, additives, all kinds of radia-

tion and low quality, mass-produced food products. It is impossible
to live and perform optimally under these conditions. We are natural beings who have evolved over billions of years in a natural world,
yet life has become incredibly complex, and life's requirements have
become equally challenging. Our nutritional demands have always
been intricate, but today our bodies are overwhelmed by the demands that our lifestyles and environment place on them.

Human beings are composed of trillions of cells, each with
unique nutritional needs. We can thrive only when all these cells
and their related systems are healthy and working together in har-
mony. Sound nutrition to all areas of the body, including those
aspects which compose our mind and spirit, is critical. However,
modern nutrition is extremely limited and lacking in many trace
nutrients that the body, mind and spirit need and crave. Since the
foods we eat support a multitude of functions and help our bodies
defend themselves against the environmental dangers that we constantly face, specialized nutritional supplementation has become a
must . . .

[*Source of Life*]–Liquid Mineral Complex is a concentrated liquid
blend of all 84 minerals and trace elements, extracted and purified
from the Great Inland Sea. The human body needs every one of
these 84 trace elements to function properly. Since all life came
from the sea, and human blood is virtually identical in its mineral
content to sea water, our blood is a means of maintaining the original environment of the sea within our bodies. However, current
nutrition is grossly lacking in most of these minerals, and as a result
most people suffer a variety of problems from trace mineral deficiencies. . . . Take 1/2 teaspoon (40 drops) once daily or 1/4 teaspoon (20 drops) twice daily. Mix with filtered water, fresh carrot
juice, tomato juice or fruit juice. [Extracted from advertising ma-
terials]

Research Methods and Results

Forty-two subjects agreed to participate in a study to determine
the effectiveness of the "Source of Life" mineral supplement. Tim
claimed that the supplement would increase one's level of energy,
help one to think more clearly, improve one's overall sense of well-
being, and aid one's work efficiency and ability to stay task-oriented.
Questions tapping subjects' performance in each of these four domains were developed for this evaluation study. Responses to each

question ranged from a negative pole of "1" (e.g., very lethargic, very inefficient at work) to a positive pole of "10" (e.g., very energetic, excellent efficiency at work). Subjects responded to the four questions four days prior to the intervention phase of the study (baseline measure) and at the end of each of the five intervention days. Finally, prior to the study each subject rated the overall nutritional adequacy of her or his diet from "1" (very inadequate) to "10" (excellent). This last rating was included as a possible covariate, as "Source of Life" might be expected to result in minimal positive change in affect for people who ate well-balanced diets, even if the mineral supplement was a very effective product, since such subjects would lack few needed minerals. Thus, if "Source of Life" subjects did slightly (but nonsignificantly) better than control subjects, this nutritional covariate could be entered into the analysis to provide a more sensitive and powerful picture of the nutritional supplement's effectiveness.

The forty-two subjects were randomly assigned to either a treatment or alternative control condition. Alternative control condition subjects drank a nine-ounce glass of *5-Alive* (a juice drink blending five fruit juices) each weekday morning of the intervention. This represents a very difficult control condition for "Source of Life" to compete against, as it possesses positive, psychological, placebo effects, as well as the facilitative physical effects of drinking an additional forty-five ounces of a fruit juice drink over a five-day period. Thus, it is labeled as an alternative treatment rather than as a placebo or no-treatment control group. Treatment subjects also drank the nine-ounce glass of *5-Alive* plus forty drops of "Source of Life" mineral supplement each weekday of the intervention phase of the study. The fruit juice drink was necessary to cover the taste of the mineral supplement, so that subjects would remain unaware of whether they were in the treatment or control condition. Figure 11-1 presents mean scores for treatment and control subjects on baseline and for each day of the intervention phase. These means include data across all four questions for all subjects.

As can be seen from these data, ratings from baseline to intervention phase rose slightly for treatment subjects. Unfortunately, data for alternative control subjects showed a remarkable improvement from baseline through intervention days. The fact that the lines in Figure 11-1 crossed over one another reveals that control

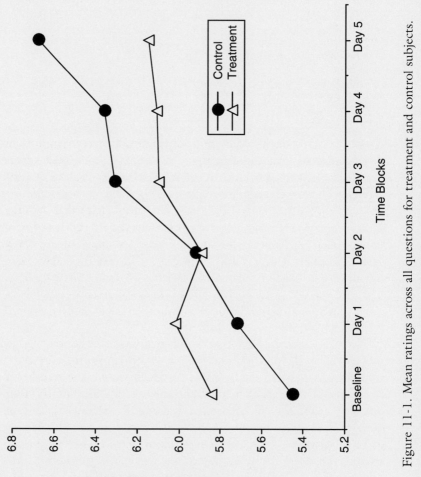

Figure 11-1. Mean ratings across all questions for treatment and control subjects.

Table 11-2
Mean scores for each outcome measure separately.

	Energy	Clear Thinking	Well-Being	Efficient & Task-Oriented
Control				
Baseline	5.20	5.45	6.00	5.15
Intervention	6.14	6.28	6.19	6.20
Treatment				
Baseline	5.04	6.18	6.45	5.68
Intervention	6.08	6.06	6.30	5.80

subjects actually improved more from baseline to intervention than their treatment group counterparts. A two-way (treatment versus control X baseline versus intervention) multivariate analysis of variance over the four questions revealed a nonsignificant interaction effect ($F(4, 37) = 1.49$, $p = .22$). Thus, we cannot claim that "Source of Life" subjects felt significantly worse than the alternative control subjects looking from baseline to intervention phases of the study even though treatment subjects' means on intervention days were actually *below* those of the control subjects. However, these findings represent terrible news for Tim and his business associates. Analyses using diet as a covariate did little to help the dismal picture painted for "Source of Life" in this study.

Table 11-2 presents the means for treatment and control group subjects for each question separately over both baseline and intervention phases of the study. While treatment subjects scored lower than control subjects over intervention days on three of the four outcome measures, this difference was not statistically significant overall. Thus, while we *cannot* assert that something about "Source of Life" actually impeded the operation of *5-Alive* when used as an alternative intervention, we cannot see any reason to purchase another bottle of Tim's elixir. By the way, "Source of Life" has eighteen other sibling formulas that are more specific to particular body deficiencies, such as reduced immune surveillance, deficient circulation, and malnourished eyes. I'll leave it to others to evaluate the efficacy of the claims of these other products.

For now, several summary observations can be made. If one

wants to be certain she or he is drinking pure water, there are some fine filters (such as the one used herein) that can remove certain water impurities. This option is much cheaper than buying bottled water. However, despite its advertising suggestions, there was no evidence of effectiveness for "Source of Life." Finally, it is extremely difficult and costly for one to know whether the claims of efficacy associated with so many products possess substance. For example, my investigations consumed several hours per week over a three-month period and cost me $576 ($200 for the filter, $18 for "Source of Life," $259 for a Hach kit, $24 for a bacterial test, and $75 for 5-Alive). Remember that U.S.D.A. approval (which "Source of Life" possesses) means that the product will not hurt you—it does not imply that the product achieves what its advertisement might suggest.

This chapter dramatizes several important ecological points. Air, water, and solid waste pollution influences each of us personally. These direct, physical threats to our health and happiness will only increase over time. Naturally, we will want to protect ourselves from these ever more toxic influences. And since money is to be made in the business of protecting people from toxic influences, not every product designed to do so will be true to its claims. What, then, is a person to do? Remain unprotected to the threats? Purchase an ecological security blanket and hope that it works? Deny that there is any reason for concern?

The dedication of this book spoke of the "wicked uncertainties" of the twenty-first century. While these uncertainties will be great, there are a few extremely cost-effective steps that can be taken now to make the problems of the future more manageable. First, it is true that an ounce of prevention is worth a pound of cure. Thus, legislation designed to lower the quantities and types of pollutants that enter our air, landfills, ground water, lakes, streams, and oceans could be strengthened. Second, the five characteristics of sustainable lifestyles (conservation, recycling, renewable resource use, restoration, and population control) might be facilitated (via business practices, legislation, social pressure, etc.) so that the flood of toxic wastes produced by current, unsustainable lifestyles will be reduced substantially. Finally, while the report card on Tim's company's products was mixed in the studies reported herein, the company strives to produce the sort of products that might be helpful for a twenty-first century plagued by wicked uncertainties and very real ecological threats. If the company takes the negative results on "Source of Life" and conducts rigorous studies that show the present findings to be misleading, or uses these negative findings to reformulate and improve its products, or eventually drops any products that can't be proven effective, then it will be serving its customers and society well. Such companies will help people to deal with ecological problems that will need to be confronted.

Imagine that I provided a copy of this chapter to Tim. What would Tim do with it? He might assume that we made a mistake in the "Source of Life" study and simply ignore the findings. Should he, instead, show the study to his bosses, and perhaps jeopardize his job? Might he take this a step further and threaten to blow the whistle on his company unless they do something about "Source of Life's" lack of effectiveness?

These are heavy issues to lay on the shoulders of a well-intentioned twenty-three year old. Would it be cheap-valor for a tenured professor to place these moral and ethical dilemmas in the lap of someone struggling to take his first steps in the business world? In fact the more I think about this quandary, the more I question whether I ought to give this chapter to Tim. What would you do?

Remember the blindnesses described in Chapter 1? Because I know Tim, I realize that he (and others in his company also) are not trying to fleece unsuspecting customers with "Source of Life." They genuinely believe that it works. I truly wish our study had turned out differently. Tim could then have sold the mineral supplement confidently—and I would have purchased it happily. But things just didn't work out that way. Apparently, the ecological problems of the coming century will not be solved quite as simply as Tim and his company had hoped. While that summary judgment might be disappointing, it represents a reality to which we ought not to turn a blind eye.

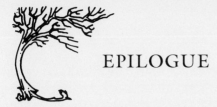

EPILOGUE

CHANGING HUMAN NATURE

CAN HUMAN NATURE be changed? I doubt seriously that cats can change their basic nature. And it is preposterous to even think that planets might choose to change their nature. Once a passive, inanimate object—mindlessly heeding gravity's commands—always a passive, inanimate object. What then leads us to think that humans might have the power to change their nature?

Before describing why and how humans might engineer changes in their basic, shared nature, we might first attempt to describe human nature itself. Drawing from various encyclopedias, the following composite description might be entertained.

> Human Beings (*Homo sapiens*): Biped, omnivorous, mammal, primate, social animal, language user, tool user, approximately 4.1 offspring, approximately 100 kg. in weight, approximately 1.8 m. in height, nine-month gestation period, warm blooded, vertebrate.

Obviously, some of these are general characteristics of humans that do not describe all people. For example, while we have the ability to be omnivorous, many people choose not to eat meat. While capable of acting as a carnivore, such people can effectively make themselves into herbivores. Have these people changed their human nature?

Humans also seem to have changed over time. Human beings now tend to average 3.6 offspring per woman. But that was not always the case. Further, fertility rates are vastly different in different locations, ranging from 1.3 children per family in Italy to 7.1 in Tanzania. Do we have different human natures in these extreme cases? Of course not! Extreme social and cultural circumstances highlight how much human behavior can be altered. Perhaps an evolutionary biologist would require changes of the magnitude where a group becomes reproductively segregated, and over time evolves into a separate species, before she or he would be willing to admit that human nature had been fundamentally altered. Thus, human nature is extremely difficult to change, if one accepts the evolutionary biologist's stringent criterion for change. However, humanity simply doesn't have the time required to engineer biological, evolutionary changes in human nature in order to escape our ecological dilemmas. Therefore, we must turn to the much speedier process of cultural evolution to consider ways to modify the most detrimental aspects of our current nature as humans if we are to engineer changes in a timely manner.

We must change ourselves—our thoughts, actions, lifestyles, dreams, and ambitions. The beacon toward which our cultural evolution should be directed is the goal of becoming a sustainable society—one that satisfies its needs without jeopardizing the prospects of future generations.

Human Engineering: Changing Our Ways of Thinking and Living

A thesis of this book is that the ecological problems of the twenty-first century will be more tractable to effective human engineering than they will be to technological breakthroughs. Recent per capita food production declines offer a good example. While agricultural breakthroughs will always help the worldwide food situation, none appears to be in the offing to solve the approaching problem of food shortages. However, two tractable pieces of human engineering could help the food situation immensely.

The first concerns our current eating habits. It requires about ten calories of vegetation to produce one calorie of meat. Thus, if we were to eat less meat we would have a tenfold (in theory, six- to sevenfold in actuality) increase in the number of vegetable calories available for consumption for each of the meat calories we forego. Health experts claim that a diet that consisted of less meat and far more grains would, in fact, be a healthier diet for Americans.

Secondly, if humans reduced their birth rate from 3.6 children per family to 2.1 children per family, the food situation would be improved dramatically. All of the birth control technologies needed to produce this reduction in birth rates are already available. Reason suggests that birth control is a humane way to avert a "death-rate solution" to the crisis of overpopulation. However, certain social institutions now keep us from fully utilizing these technological aids. For example, the Catholic Church teaches that artificial methods of contraception are wrong. Interestingly, studies repeatedly demonstrate that whenever access to artificial methods of birth control is restricted, the incidence of abortion rises. Thus, from an ecological perspective, the Catholic Church's current opposition to *both* abortion and artificial means of contraception might be seen as a fundamentally incoherent position.

Catholics believe that God's word is revealed to them through the life of Jesus (as seen in the gospels), through the history of the community of the faithful (the church), through one's experiences in struggling to be a moral person, and through humans' experience of the history of the cosmos. But the dictates of these four sources of revealed truth are not always univocal. Adjudicating inconsistencies among sources of revealed truth has become a thorny problem for numerous Catholics who struggle to make peace between these warring factions. Many Catholics (see Howard 1993b, 1994) are working to encourage the Catholic Church to change its official opposition to artificial means of birth control, as it has changed on many other issues (e.g., eating meat on Friday being sinful, any interest on loans being usury). Similarly, every religion should examine the ways that its beliefs help (or hinder) its believers in leading ecologically appropriate lifestyles. Worldwide changes in humans' atittudes about family size and eating habits could go a long way toward ameliorating possible, impending food shortages.

How Might Cultural Evolution Occur?

Books like this represent exercises in cultural evolution. Chapter 1 briefly reviewed certain blindnesses (e.g., lack of insight into the thinking of the "other," assigning monetary values to all things, overweighing short-term considerations in decision making) that contribute to the alarming ecological problems we now face. By continually showing these blindnesses at work in human action (in the intervening chapters), I hoped to improve your awareness of issues and perspectives that would suggest more ecologically benign attitudes, actions, and lifestyles.

You've probably wondered why I spoke of death so often in this book. To a psychologist, the many "blindnesses" traced in Chapter 1 represent perplexing cognitive phenomena. Why would people not "see" trends that are so obvious and ominous? Perhaps we ought to begin to wonder, "What is *gained* by remaining blind to troubling ecological trends?" For example, who paid to produce those pamphlets that trumpeted the misleading statistics about "plunging fertility rates?" By believing that exponential growth can go on forever, perhaps we enable ourselves to deny the existence of all limits—even that most psychologically important limit, our own mortality. By facing our limits with open eyes, perhaps we can become less blind (i.e., employ less denial, self-deception, etc.) to the ways that we are ruining the fragile, biological web of life on earth—the only womb capable of nurturing human life in this otherwise cold and lonely universe.

When exposed to technologies like compact florescent bulbs, geothermal heating and cooling systems, extremely fuel-efficient cars, etc., many people immediately recognize their ecological value. However, our research reveals that few consumers find themselves able to make the financial sacrifices necessary to greatly overpay (in the short run) for an ecologically and economically important (in the longer run) technology. Thus, for most people, more than a simple change in ecological awareness is required. Several parts of this book (most specifically in Chapters 8 and 10) suggest that more thoroughgoing changes in the financial lifestyles of contemporary Americans might be required for them: 1) to see themselves as investors in the future rather than consumers in the present; and 2) to have sufficient positive cash-flow from previous, smart economic decisions (e.g., "tuna money," having paid down debt) to make needed ecologically appropriate investments.

We need to see Madison Avenue's advertisement propaganda, that we adopt wasteful, consumption-oriented lifestyles, as an evil that we and our children ought to be inoculated against. In the long run, wasteful overconsumption, unbridled greed, and short-term myopia might come to be instinctively seen as destructive vices. We must work to undo the cumulative, negative effects of culturally ingrained, killer thoughts like those described in Chapter 6. If these changes occur, cultural evolution might begin to mold humans into ecologically appropriate beings.

In a revealing essay, Brown, Flavin, and Postel (1990) trace the ways in which our world in the year 2030 will be quite different from the world today. Sustainability will be the hallmark of virtually all human activities and ambitions. However, the transition from a threatened society to a lasting society will not occur unless humans first change themselves.

Movement toward a lasting society cannot occur without a transformation of individual priorities and values. Throughout the ages, philosophers and religious leaders have denounced material-ism as a viable path to human fulfillment. Yet societies across the ideological spectrum have persisted in equating quality of life with increased consumption. Personal self-worth typically is measured by possessions, just as social progress is judged by GNP growth.

Because of the strain on resources it creates, materialism simply cannot survive the transition to a sustainable world. As public un-derstanding of the need to adopt simpler and less consumptive life-styles spreads, it will become unfashionable to own fancy new cars and clothes. This shift, however, will be among the hardest to make, since consumerism so deeply permeates societies of all po-litical stripes. Yet the potential benefits of unleashing the tremen-dous quantities of human energy now devoted to designing, pro-ducing, advertising, buying, consuming, and discarding material goods are enormous. Much undoubtedly would be channeled into forming richer human relationships, stronger communities, and greater outlets for cultural diversity, music, and the arts. (p. 190)

The Challenge of Reengineering Wasteful Systems

Over time, we have *institutionalized* our wasteful and destructive attitudes by creating toxic systems (e.g., business, political, educa-tional, legal, etc.) that virtually demand that wasteful lifestyles be lived. For example, Chapter 9 demonstrates that our ability to prop-erly dispose of solid waste is enhanced (or diminished) not only by the values of the local businesses (e.g., Superior Waste Systems), but also by the changing economic and political realities that impact businesses' ability to act in an ecologically appropriate manner. In order to radically change human nature we need to reengineer the systems that serve to train and maintain our daily behaviors. Econo-mists must apprise us of the total costs (by including *all* inputs and outputs) of our current systems. The twentieth-century habit of externalizing (i.e., ignoring) real costs and effects wherever possible could only work in an underpopulated, resource-rich world that was also blessed with abundant, underused waste sinks. That world is now gone. However, the intellectual sloth, implicit in the practice of externalizing real costs, will prove lethal in the next century. The proper ecological accountancy of complex systems becomes more difficult with each passing year. However, ecological accountancy is a career field in need of honest, creative minds to correctly shepherd society through the important times and decisions that lie ahead.

Real creativity will be required to develop improved transportation, legal, business, energy, educational, marketing, and agricultural systems for the world of the future. This work will involve developing systems that operate with severely limited resources and overused waste sinks, but nonetheless service many people. Using fewer resources and producing less waste will represent the standard job-description for professionals of the twenty-first century. What a remarkable array of intellectual challenges to offer to any generation.

The American public has only recently become aware that several of our cherished social institutions have unintentionally fostered ecologically inappropriate outcomes. For example, we have recently awakened to the ways in which the tax code, the welfare system, and our immigration policies have contributed to the overpopulation of our country. These misguided (in some ways) policies were instituted in response to real problems and were energized by the good intentions by their creators. We possess a tax code that supports "family values," a welfare system that is responsive to the needs of children born into poverty, and an immigration policy that enables business to obtain cheap labor that will help American businesses to be competitive internationally. However, over time such policies make it difficult for our country to do its part toward stemming global overpopulation.

Many people are now repulsed by the destruction produced by our current business, economic, and political systems. Still, little societal change seems to be occurring. Perhaps this is because my and your attitudes, beliefs, and dreams are not yet enough well formed and well communicated to others. My experience in trying to block the repeal of the 4.3 cent gas tax was instructive. After hearing the connection between the tax and ecological issues my friends and colleagues offered their wholehearted support. However, it is very difficult to even see the evironmental impacts that our political and economic choices and policies will produce. Perhaps a bit more self-change by each of us—and many millions of Americans like us—is required to produce the sea-change necessary to begin to lead our nation into a sustainable twenty-first century. By supporting like-minded people and policies, we nurture the collective dream of a human nature and society that can live in peace with the many other citizens of the web of life. To my way of thinking, this would represent a changed—and far better—human nature in which all of us might gladly share.

Self-Change to Systems-Change to Policy-Change

This heading does *not* imply a direction in which ecological change must occur. Rather, it suggests a type of change where the professional skills and expertise of psychologists might be especially helpful. Working directly with individuals to produce change (a bottom-up approach) might be the domain where psychologists perform best. Obviously, political scientists, systems analysts, and others possess expertise and skills that are more valuable in producing top-down patterns of change. Of course, changes toward more ecologically sustainable lifestyles are welcome, regardless of how such changes are produced (top-down versus bottom-up) or maintained.

The bottom-up approach was highlighted in this book. If I can produce more ecologically appropriate attitudes in myself (Part I), I might see some practical actions that I can take to make small changes toward living a more sustainable lifestyle (Part II). I can then use whatever skills and power I might possess to influence the attitudes of other humans (e.g., writing this book, teaching ecological psychology courses). Finally, I stand ready to support and facilitate the suggestions for creating more earth-friendly systems and policies that others (e.g., politicians, economists, ecological activist groups) might create. Having read this far, I trust that you are something of a kindred spirit—an ecological soulmate. Your background, skills, and dreams are probably quite different from mine—and that's for the good. Your uniqueness enables you to strike a creative blow for ecological sanity that I can fully appreciate only after having witnessed your accomplishment. By producing millions of such acts of ecological sanity, our business and political systems will come around to this new way of thinking and being, for their very survival is dependent upon their being responsive to the will of their constituencies.

When humans learn to feel good about themselves and their ecologically appropriate actions, and when they enhance and protect (rather than stress and destroy) the entire web of life that supports human life, then people will instinctively be ecologists and preservationists.

Will our best efforts be sufficient to avert the ecological catastrophes that many have foreseen? No one knows for sure. But even if it is now too late, and our fate is already sealed, I recommend that we mend our beliefs, and strive to develop more ecologically appropriate lifestyles. This is the only morally appropriate way to lead our lives—regardless of our species' ultimate fate. James (1897) said it best, "Be strong and of good courage. Act for the best, hope for the best, and take what comes. . . . If death ends all, we cannot meet death better" (p. 31).

APPENDIX A

STUDIES OF ENERGY CONSERVATION
Experiencing Impediments to and Opportunities for Ecological Activism

PER CAPITA CONSUMPTION of energy in the United States is the highest of any country in the world (Shapiro 1992), and we are now the greatest energy wasters in the history of our planet. Recall from Chapter 4 that energy consumption is the measure of affluence and technology (AXT) in the I = PAT formula. A child born in the United States today will (on average) consume *thirty times* the energy over her or his lifetime of a comparable child born in India. Thus, even though India's birth rate is 85 percent higher than the birth rate of the United States, we stress the planet's energy resources, and its capacity to neutralize waste products, far more severely than do Indians. Thus we cannot in fairness urge Indians to curb their birth rate unless we first strive to minimize our excessive use of the planet's nonrenewable energy resources. Brown, Flavin and Postel (1991) state the challenge to Americans boldly,

> . . . a sustainable world economy, therefore, cannot be primarily powered by oil and coal. The easiest, fastest, and cheapest way to reduce reliance on these fuels is to use energy more efficiently— that is, to do more with less. By using new technologies to make homes more weather-tight, automobiles more economical in their use of fuel, and stoves more efficient, energy needs can be reduced while the growing needs of people are met. Although advancing technology has yielded steady efficiency gains throughout the past century, this process needs to be accelerated if we are to reduce fossil fuel use sufficiently to stabilize the climate. (pp. 35–36)

Countless hours are spent in college classrooms discussing the troubled ecological state of our world. But rarely do these discussions lead to programs of action that influence the course of an ecological threat. A group of psychology students at the University of Notre Dame were galvanized into action by the realization that every compact fluorescent bulb put into service will, over its lifetime, save the burning of one ton of coal (Gore 1992, p. 332). This appendix demonstrates the step-by-step program of research, first referred to in Chapter 5, that was designed to replace energy inefficient incandescent light bulbs with high efficiency fluorescent light bulbs. The program furnishes the reader with all of the information and techniques required to implement the program in his or her own community. Doing so could multiply the environmental benefits documented herein hundreds of times over. Further, students who conduct such programs learn a good deal about the problems associated with changing consumers' behavior; strategies for implementing change programs in complex organizations; and the trials and tribulations of working toward the reversal of dangerous ecological trends (e.g., carbon dioxide buildup, smog, acid rain) that now threaten our planet. Finally, students experience the satisfaction of converting personal values into concrete programs of action that honor those values.

Caring for a Sick Earth—And Making Money in the Process

Table A-1 takes the reader through a cost–effectiveness analysis of replacing 100 watt incandescent light bulbs with 20 watt fluorescent bulbs in reading lamps in students' dormitory rooms at Notre Dame. As Vice President Gore suggested, our tests reveal that both yield equivalent amounts of light. In a totally dark room, both bulbs yield about 43 foot–candles of illumination. Our government recommends that 35 foot–candles are sufficient for reading a book.

The fluorescent bulb lasts at least ten times as long as an incandescent bulb, so the cost of ten old bulbs would be $5.00 (this price reflects Notre Dame's bulk purchase rate). We thought that Notre Dame would save $5.76 in electricity costs per year for each fluorescent bulb placed in service. Dormitory usage rates suggest the fluorescent bulb will last 5.5 years. Thus, had Notre Dame remained with incandescent bulbs it would have spent $36.68 (materials +

Table A-1
Cost-Efficiency of Changing from a 100 W Incandescent to a
20 W Fluorescent Bulb in Notre Dame Dormitories

Usage: 6 hrs./day × 300 days/year = 1800 hrs./yr.
Energy savings: 100 W − 20 W = 80 W savings × 1800 hrs./yr = 144
  kW hrs./yr.
Cost savings for electricity: 144 kW/yr. × $.04/kW hr. ND electric rate =
  $5.76/yr.
Life of old bulb = 1,000 hrs.; life of new bulb = 10,000 hrs.: 10 old
  bulbs = 1 new bulb,
Life of new bulb: 10,000 hrs. @ 1800 hrs./yr. usage = 5.5 years
Cost-efficient Price of New Bulb = 10 (.50) + 5.5 ($5.90/yr.) = $36.68

Note: Notre Dame's electricity rate of $.04 per kW hr. (on line 3) is astonishingly
low because the University purchases modest amounts of power at low commercial rates. Notre Dame's power plant then produces all of the power it needs at
peak demand times (7 A.M. to 7 P.M., weekdays). This demand pattern merits
Indiana & Michigan Power Company's most favorable rate—often less than $.02
per kW hr.

additional energy expenditures) over that 5.5 year period. Notre
Dame's cost for the fluorescent bulb was $14.50 (again, bulk rate
for an item that retailed for $24.50). Over 2,000 fluorescent bulbs
were placed in service in Notre Dame dormitories from July 1992
to November 1992 to document the hoped-for electricity savings.
The results of this study are reported below.

Study 1: The Energy Efficiency of Compact Fluorescent Bulbs

Notre Dame's Executive Vice President agreed to spend $29,000
to purchase 2,000 compact fluorescent bulbs for a pilot study to
document the energy savings promised by the bulb manufacturers.
[This level of support by the University Administration was quite
shocking—since we had originally asked for only $1,500.] If it
could be demonstrated that Notre Dame would not lose money on
the project, all incandescent bulbs on campus would then be replaced as soon as monies could be freed up to cover the high initial
cost of the high efficiency lighting.

Ten dormitories were selected to participate in this study. Dormitories were paired with neighboring dormitories of equal age, ar-

chitecture, and student characteristics. For each couplet, assignment to treatment or control conditions of one member of the dormitory pair was done randomly. The data for these ten dormitories are presented in Figure A-1.

Wherever possible, all incandescent bulbs were replaced by compact fluorescent bulbs in the five treatment dormitories in August 1992. Thus, the left panel of Figure A-1 presents the average 1991 electricity consumption in three target months for the two sets of dormitories as baseline data. The treatment dormitories are designated as Xs, while the control dormitories are represented by Os. The right panel presents data on average electricity consumption for treatment and control dormitories for the same months in 1992— after the fluorescent bulbs had been installed in the five treatment dormitories. Based upon the 1991 data, and the 1992 data for the control dormitories, one can easily calculate the expected 1992 electricity consumption for the treatment dormitories, *if the incandescent bulbs had not been replaced,* by solving the following proportion:

$$\frac{1991 \text{ Control}}{1991 \text{ Treatment}} = \frac{1992 \text{ Control}}{1992 \text{ Expected Consumption}}$$

The data for the computation of the September-November 1992 expected value for experimental dormitories were

$$\frac{32,000 \text{ kW. hrs.}}{30,300 \text{ kW. hrs.}} = \frac{34,600 \text{ kW. hrs.}}{1992 \text{ Expected Consumption/month/dormitory}}$$

yielding an expected value of 32,760 kW. hrs./month for the experimental dormitories. Thus, an average of 2,750 kW. hrs./month/dormitory was saved by the new bulbs. By dividing these energy savings by the average number of compact fluorescent bulbs in the experimental dormitories, one arrives at an estimate of the electricity savings per month per bulb. By multiplying those estimates by $.04 (Notre Dame's electricity cost per kilowatt hour) one arrives at an estimate of monthly energy savings per bulb of $2.30 (lights in dormitories were lit for far more hours per day than we had anticipated, which led to the high monthly savings.) Thus, Notre Dame recovers its high capital outlay ($14.50 per bulb) *in energy savings alone* in less than seven months. The remaining years of bulb life and energy savings are pure profit. The ecological benefits of the

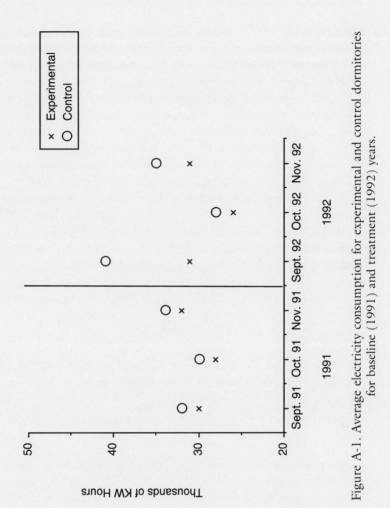

Figure A-1. Average electricity consumption for experimental and control dormitories for baseline (1991) and treatment (1992) years.

changeover further attest to the fact that such programs can be both economically valuable *and* ecologically appropriate. The University replaced 8,000 incandescent bulbs with compact fluorescent bulbs by August 1994. Between then and February 1997, the University will have saved in excess of $190,000 because of this project.

Appendix B presents two studies that consider marketing strategies to enhance the acceptance of (i.e., willingness to purchase) energy efficient fluorescent bulbs for use in private residences. The two studies found that teaching people about the economic and ecological value of these bulbs and giving them a brief opportunity to test them out at home will lead them to purchase modest numbers of compact fluorescents. Members of higher income groups purchase more bulbs than lower income group subjects, as they have less disposable income. Because of the studies reported in this Appendix and in Appendix B, a bit more was learned about how we all might become a bit more ecologically responsible. But, equally importantly, we were able (through these efforts) to make small changes in our world. While these first steps were small and halting, we now have some momentum behind us. Lastly, what we accomplished required no special skills on our part. Any psychologist—and her or his students—are perfectly capable of accomplishing what we did, and far more.

Impediments to Ecological Activism

Had I known four years ago all the obstacles that stood in the way of making Notre Dame and South Bend a little more energy efficient, I doubt that I would have chosen to become involved at all. The forces deployed against such institutional change are staggering. Invoking battle imagery in the last sentence is not being overly dramatic because effecting real change in this world inevitably thrusts us into struggles over "turf." Notre Dame employs a flock of engineers, electricians, physical plant managers, purchasing supervisors, and facilities administrators all of whose professional expertise and competence might be seen as being questioned when some chuckle-headed psychologist announces that Notre Dame could be more energy efficient, and thus inflict less air pollution upon the planet. After all, how do psychologists feel when, for example, some accountant asserts that psychotherapy doesn't work, and thus is a waste of time and money? Or what do I think when someone's cousin tells me that psychological research is so "soft" that it can't be thought of as "real" science? Fairness demands that most of us recognize that we are amateur electricians, ecologists, and political activists, and thus (in a sense) practicing outside our area of competence. Obviously, I believe we should press on in our ecological activist efforts, but we really can't expect to be welcomed onto other professionals' turf with open arms.

Put Your Money (and Time, and Energy) Where Your Values Are!

How can psychologists make small but significant contributions in the fight toward ecological sanity? It turns out that actions on a variety of levels can sum to yield important effects. Take my experience as a case in point. The chapters in Part II demonstrate that there are a variety of ways that each psychologist can become involved in the battle to save our planet.

The two studies in Appendix B on residential purchases of compact fluorescents did not reveal incentives that produced large numbers of sales. Can some psychologist out there figure out a feasible incentive plan that will entice homeowners to convert the majority of their light bulbs at home to genuinely high efficiency lighting devices? Once that incentive system's effectiveness has been documented, that person will have rendered our world an inestimable service—not to mention having given her or his own career a tremendous boost.

In all likelihood it is the high initial cost of energy-saving devices that keeps consumers from honoring their ecological values and purchasing these products. But as the sales volume of such devices increases, their unit cost decreases. Thus, there will come a point where the unit cost is sufficiently low that consumers will freely purchase such devices solely because their economic and ecological values overwhelm the resistance due to (the now lower) initial cost. Analogously, if one wished to remove the earthen dam of consumer resistance to investing in energy-conserving devices, it might not be necessary to demolish the entire dam. By starting a trickle of purchases, this tiny stream will eat away at the dam itself (a trickle of sales lowers unit costs which then stimulates further sales). By enlarging its own breech, a trickle might in time collapse a dam of resistance. With this hope in mind, we might learn to be content with numerous small gains, rather than becoming discouraged because we don't see dramatic successes.

But the impact of our ecological efforts goes far beyond dormitory and residential conservation programs. Most psychologists are professionals who are engaged in a variety of attitude change activities. This is true whether one's primary job title is teacher, clinician, consultant, or researcher. I now teach courses in ecological psychology—whereas three years ago I didn't. My reading recommendations to friends, relatives, colleagues, students, and local politicians now have titles like *Earth in the Balance* (Gore 1992), *Saving the Planet* (Brown, Flavin, and Postel 1991), *The Politics of the Solar Age* (Henderson 1981), *The Voice of the Earth* (Roszak 1992), *The Ecology of Commerce* (Hawken 1993), *How Much Is Enough?* (Durning 1992), and *The Population Explosion* (Ehrlich and Ehrlich 1990). I now suggest that topics for good senior honors theses, specialty papers, masters and doctoral theses can be found lurking in the pages of the *Handbook of Environmental Psychology* (Stokols and Altman 1987). Will these tiny rivulets eventually sum to a current of substance? I certainly hope they will; and I firmly believe they will if each of us decides to act as a multiplier of the impulses that nudge us to invest our time, energy, and money in the interests of promoting ecological sanity.

Having indicated that my time and energy are invested in the fight for a sustainable world, you might wonder whether my money is also behind my values. One does not work in the ecological psychology area long before realizing that money is a root of our ecological difficulties—and the chief stumbling block to implementing putative solutions. While I could easily demonstrate how high efficiency lighting devices would eventually save Notre Dame and local homeowners money, someone had to ante up the initial $30,000 required to get the projects rolling (The purchase of the compact fluorescent bulbs being the single largest cost.) The last delay of the Notre Dame dormitory project was simply waiting for the advent of the new budget year—as there simply was no more money in the prior year's till. I was forced to put up $5,000 of my own money to see that the residential project was run. I hope to have my money returned eventually. I mention this fact to warn you that while everyone praises conservation projects, unless someone steps forward to underwrite their costs, they are as dead as doornails. Ultimately, you might be forced to pay up, or see your efforts to that point go wasted.

There are other ways that one can put their money behind their ecological values. My high efficiency gas furnace broke a few years ago, and I looked into replacing it with a much higher efficiency geothermal unit (where heat and cooling are taken from the earth, rather than produced by burning nonrenewable natural resources and further polluting our air). A five-ton geothermal unit costs about $3,000 more than a replacement gas furnace initially, but I more than recovered that investment in natural gas and electricity savings in a few years. Indiana and Michigan Power (I&M) further enticed me to make the environmentally correct choice by giving me a grant of $115 per ton of geothermal capacity as part of their residential, demand-side management program. Later, in Appendix C, I'll analyze exactly who pays for the $575 incentive that I received from I&M.

Does My Geothermal Unit Save Energy?

Psychology's commitment to science prods us to demonstrate a program's effectiveness before we recommend it as a course of action to others. Thus, I asked I&M to supply me with the electricity consumption records of five of my neighbors whose electricity consumption for the summer of 1991 approximated my level of use. None of these neighbors availed themselves of demand-side incentives for energy conservation. Figure A-2 presents (in the left panel) my electricity consumption for the three summer months of 1991 and the average of my nonequivalent control group neighbors for the same months. Control subjects consumed about 100 kW hrs. per month more electricity for the summer of 1991 than did I (Control M = 1737; Treatment M = 1632).

Data for the summer of 1992 can be found in the far righthand panel of Figure A-2. Using the summer of 1991 data and the control subjects' summer 1992 data, my expected use of electricity can be ascertained via the following proportion,

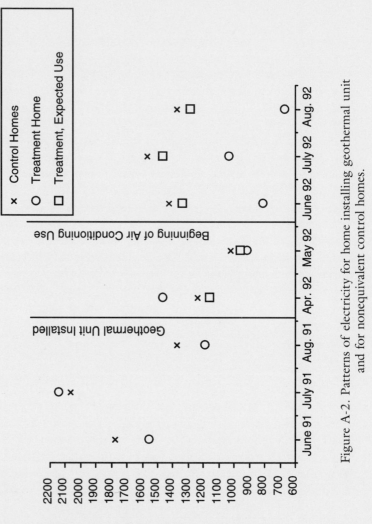

Figure A-2. Patterns of electricity for home installing geothermal unit and for nonequivalent control homes.

$$\frac{\text{Month 1991 Control}}{\text{Month 1991 Treatment}} = \frac{\text{Month 1992 Control}}{\text{Month 1992 Expected}}$$
(Treatment)

and these expected consumption values are depicted by squares in Figure A-2. One can see that my summer 1992 electricity consumption was about 550 kW hrs. per month less than would have been expected had I not installed the geothermal cooling system.

Are there other rival hypotheses to the conclusion that the drop in my summer 1992 electricity consumption was due to the installation of the geothermal cooling system? The problem with nonequivalent control group designs is that some factor (such as commitment to conserving energy) might have led me (but not my neighbors) to purchase the geothermal unit, and this nonequivalence might lead me to behave differently from control subjects in other ways (e.g., turning off lights, only running a dishwasher with a full load) that would also affect the dependent measure.

To my knowledge, no other nonequivalent control group study has been able to provide data to support the equivalence of the treatment and control group. But this study is unique in that while the geothermal unit was installed in March 1992, it would not be expected to have had any impact on electricity consumption until my June 1992 bill. If I were more conservation-oriented than my control group counterparts, it should show up as lower electricity consumption in my spring 1992 bills in Figure A-2 (middle panel). In fact, just the opposite effect occurred in that my average spring electricity consumption was over 180 kW hrs. per month *greater* than my expected use. The present study provides evidence that group nonequivalence is *not* the most plausible hypothesis for my low summer 1992 consumption because of a unique feature of this study. It is rare that an intervention implemented in March can be assumed to *not* impact the dependent measure immediately, but will be expected to produce an effect at a specified point in time several months later.

While my summer electricity savings are noteworthy, they will pale in comparison with the drop in my natural gas bills for the eight months of the year when heating is required in northern Indiana. The data for this study were presented to highlight the fact that making the right choices from an ecological perspective can also represent a wise investment. Not only will my investment be repaid in less than four years, I also exchanged a sixteen-year-old central air conditioning system for a new geothermal cooling system. But the cost of a new air conditioning system was not entered into my payback calculations. (I simply considered the cost of a replacement gas furnace, the I&M rebate, and the subsequent energy savings.) If my old air conditioner had broken in June 1992 (an unknowable event), then the payback on my geothermal unit would have been only a few months. All energy savings for the remainder of the geothermal unit's forty- to fifty-year expected, usable life would then represent pure profit.

But there still remains the common misunderstanding that conservation efforts (and preserving the ecology of our world) involve making economic sacrifices. That belief is often false—and with each passing day it becomes truer that our choices to *not* conserve will cost us even more money. Appendix C demonstrates how actions designed to reduce your consumption of electricity will lower your electricity bill—that much is simple common sense. But what is surprising is that when conservation programs are offered, your electricity bill will actually *increase* (even if your consumption of electricity remains unchanged) if you decide *not* to take part in the conservation programs.

Appendix C is an example of a conceptual analysis (or a thought experiment) of the problem, "Who pays for utility-sponsored conservation programs?" I've asked this question of dozens of utility administrators and demand-side management experts. All give the answer offered in all of their textbooks. That is, since utility rates rise equally for all customers, it is claimed, all share equally in demand-side programs, just as we share equally in the cost of supply-side initiatives (such as when additional generating capacity is constructed). I believe that their standard answer is completely wrong—and that this misconception results in serious discrimination against the poor.

Given psychologists' historical role in identifying discrimination due to race, gender, lifestyles, and the like, it is not surprising that the sensitized eye of a psychologist might see economic discrimination (in the name of ecological activism) where legions of legislators, economists, engineers, bureaucrats, and others have insisted that justice for all is being served. Do psychologists have a role to play in moving toward ecological sanity, it's been asked? In fact, the closer one looks, the more apparent it becomes that psychologists are eminently well prepared to strike effective blows in this cause.

Why Should Psychologists Get Involved?

Ecologists and environmental activists are in great need of the help of psychologists. It was a comforting fantasy for humans to see the looming ecological crises as simply problems of biology and/ or applied engineering that would soon be solved by some (as yet undiscovered) biological/technological *deus ex machina*. But ecological problems run far deeper than this fantasy maintains—the problems reside within each of us. Gore (1992) sees our ecologically unsustainable lifestyles as evidence of a deeper, more pervasive malady—a "crisis of the human spirit." Gore might easily have called it a "crisis of the human psyche," and his analysis would lose none of its cogency. But before psychologists can help others in the ecological domain, they must be certain that they have addressed the malady in themselves. One ambition of the present collection of essays has been to entice psychologists to examine their own ecological consciences—for if each of us is not part of a solution to pressing ecological problems, then we are probably part of the problem.

However, psychologists are far more than merely Doctors of the Soul—to borrow Viktor Frankl's felicitous phrase. In Chapter 2 on world overpopulation, and in the thought experiment on who pays for demand side programs (Appendix C), I tried to demonstrate that (with the possible exception of a few philosophers) psychologists are as capable of helpful conceptual analysis of problems as any other group of specialists. Similarly, the studies on selling compact fluorescent bulbs and measuring their energy savings should suggest that psychologists are as capable at research methodology and program evaluation as anyone (again, with the exception of a handful of professional methodologists and program evaluation experts).

While I personally have no accomplishments in the domain of political action to cite, I can easily think of more than two dozen psychologists who showed great political acumen and organizational savvy in their fights against sexism, racism, homophobia, and in the battles over credentialing and equal access to training and research funding. The fight to save our planet will require political activism and leadership in organizing widespread societal change. Psychologists are skilled and seasoned in such struggles, and they represent valuable resources to the ecology movement.

Many of the technological solutions (birth control devices, high efficiency bulbs, recycling programs, pollution control technologies, high efficiency mass transit techniques, genetically engineered fast growing trees, etc.) to our ecological problems are now available or are in the offing. The problem is that we lack the *will* to implement these solutions. What our planet requires is a revolution in psychology—a thorough alteration of attitudes and lifestyles—that will move our species away from the insane trajectory along which we now travel. Whatever clinical skills I may once have developed as a graduate student have rusted and atrophied years ago. So personally I might be of little help in the task of working with people who experience great personal difficulty in making the transition to a more environmentally sustainable lifestyle. But, luckily, there are thousands of practitioners who are perfectly prepared to be of assistance in helping individuals and groups change their ecologically unsustainable lifestyles (see Roszak, Gomes, and Kanner 1995).

Finally, psychology's traditional emphasis on prevention, its psychoeducator models of training and change, and its predilection for healthy models of growth and development (cf. Rogers 1961; Schultz 1977) serve us well in the range of ecopsychology activities in which we might choose to become involved. We psychologists are generally an altruistic, activist, and pragmatic crowd. In this regard we share William James's vision of the world, human nature, and the meaning of life (Cotkin 1990; Howard 1992b). Because of our scientist-practitioner approach, we tend to see knowledge as *activity*, not as a product of contemplation, in which "theories become instruments, not answers to enigmas in which we can rest. We don't lie back upon them, we move forward, and on occasion *make nature over* again by their aid" (James 1920, p. 380). James claimed that pragmatists act upon *funded knowledge*—knowledge whose chief claim to truth lies in the fact that it is useful and functional ("funded" means it is based upon both common sense and scientific inquiries). Psychologists are experts in the process of coping—a phenomenon that combines elements of knowledge, action, and hope. James claimed that if there is a truth about human nature, then one cannot come to know it solely through detached, dispassionate observation. Insights into human nature will be gleaned by studying acts of self-creation—by accompanying people as they devise ways of (in James's phrase) *being good at being human.* Thus, most applied psychologists practice a philosophy of pragmatism, whether or not they are explicitly aware of doing so. But it is precisely our activist orientation, I believe, that positions psychologists to make remarkable contributions to the healing of our unsustainable beliefs and lifestyles.

While I have not focused upon the scholarly literatures in environmental science and environmental psychology in these essays, these bodies of knowledge have much to offer to psychologists' total understanding of the problems and possibilities we now face. G. T. Miller's (1993) magnificent textbook on environmental science provides perspicacious summaries of the background one needs on population demographics, physics, chemistry, engineering, and technological aspects of pollution and its amelioration, deforestation, ozone depletion, and the like. Similarly, recent, fine analyses of the research literatures in ecological psychology (e.g., on energy conservation, recycling, public policy) have been offered by Archer, Pettigrew, and Aronson (1992), Kempton, Darley, and Stern (1992), Stern (1992a, 1992b), and Gardner and Stern (1996). A general familiarity with these literatures can be achieved rather quickly (in several months) and serve to round out a person's understanding of the scope of the problems involved, and possibilities for solutions that are presently available. Finally, there are some excellent videotape series that are available through most public and university libraries that offer students a graphic overview of current ecological problems and putative solutions. Two of the best are the Corporation for Public Broadcasting's (1990) series entitled *Race to Save the Planet* and James Burke's (1987) analysis of the global warming problem called *After the Warming.* The sources cited in this paragraph, along with Ehrlich and Ehrlich (1992), Durning (1992), and the present collection of essays, could form the core of a course in ecopsychology.

How Might You Begin to Become Involved?

Perhaps you might try to get incandescent bulbs replaced in your home and place of work. Is your furnace or air conditioning unit growing old? Call your local utility and ask them about the demand-

side initiative programs they now offer. A conversation that begins
with geothermal units and thermal storage techniques could lead
into talk of weatherizing programs, high efficiency lighting, and energy efficient major appliances. If your utility says that it does not
have any demand-side initiatives, ask for the address of your state
utility regulatory commission and indicate that you intend to write
your commission (and every politician within earshot) to express
your astonishment and dismay. Would you be surprised to find that
your utility might be thrilled by the prospect of concerned citizens
pressuring their elected officials to do the right thing? If your utility
has demand-side initiatives, are the incentives uniform for all residents? You might do your utility the service of letting its officials
know that such practices are discriminatory, as poor people are un-
able to take advantage of such initiatives, but still must bear the
lion's share of the cost of such programs (as shown in Appendices B
and C). You could volunteer to study what levels of enhanced initiatives would be necessary in order to bring participation by poor
people up to the levels at which richer people participate in demand-
side management programs. That line of research would represent
a fantastic contribution to the public policy field.

You could initiate conversations with colleagues, students, con-
sultees, clients, friends, and neighbors about the ecological crises
looming before us. Let all of your elected representatives know that
you are deeply disturbed by our country's role in global overpopulation trends, per capita energy consumption in this country, our
refusal to participate in global treaties to curb the production of
greenhouse gases, and so forth. If your conscience allows, make a
contribution to Planned Parenthood International. Many of the examples in my courses on research methodology, consultation, program evaluation, philosophical psychology, and narrative psychology
now involve issues of ecology and activist responses to the deterio-
rating quality of life on our planet. Are there professional contexts
where you could introduce your ecological concerns?

Invest in companies that produce energy-saving technologies,
contraceptive devices, recycling and reuse programs, manufacturers
of wind, solar, tide, and geothermal energy technologies, forestry
companies with responsible cutting and replanting procedures, and
the like. Then go out immediately and push your companies' products as hard as you are able. If you first make your money follow

your values, you have greatly enhanced the chances that your actions will follow both—to the benefit of you, your investment, the planet, and all human beings.

One could go on and on enumerating thousands of ways that each of us might strike a small blow for ecological sanity, but I'm afraid you've probably heard enough for now. As time is a declining resource in the fight to save mother earth, space represents a resource that constrains what any writer can offer. We'd better get used to living with declining resources in virtually all domains, or bite the bullet and reduce the number of people among whom those resources must be shared, or else we are condemned to live with the inevitable, tragic consequences of having chosen to do neither. So, friends, of the many ways that I've suggested that you might befriend the earth and future generations, with which would you like to begin?

APPENDIX B

SELLING COMPACT FLUORESCENT LIGHT BULBS

TABLE B-1 presents the cost effectiveness breakdown of replacing a 100 watt incandescent bulb with a 20 watt fluorescent bulb in the South Bend area. This sort of information was presented to all subjects in the two subsequent studies to suggest the cost-savings they might realize over the life of the compact fluorescent bulb. This table also demonstrates that while materials costs of the fluorescent bulb are higher ($24 versus $8.60) this difference is more than compensated for by the fluorescents' miniscule energy costs ($16.67 versus $80). (For home owners who wish to replace 75 watt [or 60 watt] incandescent bulbs, our recommendations are the 15 watt [or 11 watt] compact fluorescent bulbs, respectively.)

Study 1: Visits to the Home: Labor Intensive, But Perhaps Extremely Effective

Method

In this study, three students and I canvassed all homes in selected neighborhoods (stratified by socio-economic status) in the South Bend/Mishawaka/Granger area of Northern Indiana. We purposely employed experimenters with a wide range of education levels (doctorate, graduate student, undergraduate, high school). Somewhat surprisingly, no differences in number of bulbs sold by the four experimenters were apparent.

The procedure in 1992 for obtaining compact fluorescent bulbs for use in residential homes was to locate a grocery, department, or building materials store that sold them (often a very difficult task); purchase the lighting device, and return home to see whether or not the new bulb fit (since the bulb portion possessed an atypical shape,

Table B-1

Cost Effectiveness for Residential Use of 20 Watt
Fluorescent Bulb in Place of 100 Watt Incandescent Bulb

	100 Watt Incandescent	20 Watt Fluorescent
Bulb life	1,000 hrs.	10,000 hrs.
Cost of bulbs over life of fluorescent	10 (.86) = $8.60	$24.50
Electricity costs over life of bulbs	100 W × 10,000 hrs. = 1,000 kW. hrs.	20W × 10,000 = 200 kW. hrs.
	1,000 kW. hrs. × $.065 (South Bend rate) = $65.00	200 kW. hrs. × $.065 (South Bend rate) = $13.00
Total Cost	$8.60 + $65.00 = $73.60	$24.50 + 13.00 = 37.50
Net Savings (realized gradually over the life of each bulb)		$36.10

Note: South Bend's residential electricity rate of .065/kW. hr. is one of the lowest
in the nation. The average electricity rate nationwide is .08 kW. hr. At that rate the
electricity cost of the old 100 watt incandescent bulbs would be $80, and the net
per bulb savings to you would be $48.10!

fluorescent bulbs frequently did not fit in fixtures—this problem of
bulb shape has been almost eliminated by 1995). The lowest retail
price we found locally was $20 per bulb for a compact fluorescent
with an electronic ballast (some cheaper compact fluorescent bulbs
have electromagnetic ballasts—but we do not recommend them as
they bring technical drawbacks such as harmonics). Thus, we elected
to sell any wattage compact fluorescent for $20 in this study. Since
the retail sale of compact fluorescent bulbs had been a commercial
failure for several years, our study considered the effect of a series
of incentives (i.e., bringing the bulb to the consumer; one week of
free home use of the bulb; and a 20 percent discount on the price
of the bulb) on sales of compact fluorescent bulbs. Subjects were
recruited into three separate income-level groups (lower, less than
$25,000 in annual family income; middle, $25,000 to $50,000 in-

come; and higher, greater than $50,000 annual income). All sub-
jects received all three incentives in the same order.

Three hundred and eighty-one homes were approached to ask
families to participate in the study. For over half of the homes, no
one even answered the door. Eventually, families in 30 percent of
the homes approached agreed to participate. A brief (ten to fifteen
minute) explanation of the economic and ecological benefits of high
efficiency lighting was followed by the offer to sell the subject as
many bulbs as he or she desired at $20 per bulb (Dependent Mea-
sure 1). All subjects were then encouraged to take a bulb for a one
week trial without obligation to purchase (66 percent of the subjects agreed to do so). Subjects who purchased a bulb on Dependent
Measure 1 were offered another bulb (of different wattage) for their
free trial. Approximately one week later the experimenter returned
to each home and asked if the subject wished to purchase additional
bulbs (Dependent Measure 2). Finally, as a way thanking subjects
for agreeing to participate in this study, we offered to sell the subject
as many bulbs as he or she desired at a 20 percent discount—$16
(Dependent Measure 3).

Results

Table B-2 shows the mean number of bulbs purchased by subjects
in the three income groups on the three dependent measures, and
the average over all of the measures (Total). Of the 480 data points
in this study (120 subjects on three dependent measures and a total
score), 0, 1, 2, and 3 bulbs purchased were the only values obtained
(and 98 percent of the values were either 0 or 1). The assumption

Table B-2
Average Number of Fluorescent Bulbs Bought at Each Stage
of the Study for Three Income Groups

Income Group	Measure 1 (bulbs per subject)	Measure 2 (bulbs per subject)	Measure 3 (bulbs per subject)	Total Purchases (bulbs per subject)
Lower	.03	.08	.13	.23
Middle	.03	.10	.00	.13
Higher	.23	.10	.03	.35

of statistical normality required for the use of parametric statistics was clearly violated. Thus, nonparametric statistics were indicated.

Overall, nineteen subjects purchased one bulb; three subjects purchased two bulbs; and one subject purchased three bulbs.

Significantly more higher income subjects purchased bulbs than did middle or lower income subjects on Dependent Measure 1 (λ^2 (2) = 10.69; p < .01). Thus, economic and ecological information, and the convenience of an in-home presentation, led eight out of forty higher income subjects to buy nine bulbs, whereas only two bulbs were bought by the other eighty subjects at that time. The one-week free home use incentive resulted in ten more sales, which were about equally divided among the three income groups (λ^2 (2) = .18; n.s.). The 20 percent discount led to six additional bulb sales with the lower income group availing themselves of disproportionately more purchases than either of the other income groups (λ^2 (2) = 5.35; .10 > p > .05). Finally, there was no difference among income groups on the Total measure of bulbs purchased (λ^2 (2) = 3.01; n. s.).

It should be noted that experimenters worked for about ninety hours to gather the data in this study. The purchase of only twenty-eight bulbs, while extremely disappointing, reinforced the common claim by manufacturers of compact fluorescent lighting that the American public is simply unwilling to spend $20 (or even $16!) for a light bulb. This reluctance to choose an *economically and ecologically* appropriate course of action was in spite of the presence of other sales incentives (the convenience of an in-home demonstration, one-week free trial use)

Study 2: Persuading Preexisting Groups to Adopt Fluorescent Bulbs for Home Use

Method

The authors recruited nine preexisting groups (e.g., all employees of a few departments at Notre Dame; workers at a restaurant; employees at the police department) who were asked to listen to a ten to twenty minute presentation on the economic efficiency and ecological value of replacing incandescent bulbs with fluorescent bulbs for home use. After participating in the brief presentation, subjects were offered the opportunity to buy fluorescent light bulbs at retail cost (Dependent Measure 1). As in Study 1, a week of free usage of the bulb preceded Dependent Measure 2, and lastly, all participants were offered the opportunity to purchase any number of bulbs at a 20 percent discount (Dependent Measure 3). The major differences between this study and Study 1 were that sales contacts were made with groups of potential customers rather than individually, and that the discussions of the bulbs took longer than in the previous study. This is because group members were stimulated by the questions and comments of other group members as well as by spontaneous testimonials by colleagues (e.g., "I read about the energy savings of these bulbs in *Consumer Reports*," "My neighbor has one and she really likes it") which seemed to increase the overall credibility of the presenters and the products. Because these initial presentations were made to groups we were able to work with subjects in about 50 percent of the time and effort required for Study 2. Because of scheduling problems, the second contact with each subject was made individually (a week after the group presentation) to retrieve the free trial use bulb and to offer the final incentive (a 20 percent discount on the price of bulbs). The critical question was: Will subjects buy the same number of bulbs with a group sales procedure, even though they will not experience the convenience of immediately seeing the bulbs demonstrated in their own homes?"

Results

Table B-3 presents the mean number of bulbs purchased per employee for each income group on each of the three dependent measures.

Table B-3
Average Number of Fluorescent Bulbs Bought at Each Stage of Study Two for the Three Income Groups

Income Group	Measure 1 (bulbs per subject)	Measure 2 (bulbs per subject)	Measure 3 (bulbs per subject)	Total Purchases (bulbs per subject)
Lower	.03	.10	.07	.21
Middle	.08	.60	.30	.98
Higher	.21	.63	.33	1.17

The data in Table B-3 are directly comparable to those in Table B-2 with the most salient difference being that the initial presentation was made in a group setting. Unlike Study 1, there were no differences in the incidence of purchasing bulbs by subjects in the various income groups on Dependent Measure 1 (λ^2 (2) = .64 ; n.s). Economic and ecological information presented in a group setting led two out of twenty-four higher income subjects to buy five bulbs, whereas only four bulbs were purchased by the other sixty-eight subjects in the study. The level of purchasing activity on Dependent Measure 1 in the present study (mean sales per subject = .10 bulbs) was about the same as in the previous study (mean sales per subject = .09 bulbs).

The one-week free home use incentive resulted in the sale of forty-two additional bulbs, which were purchased significantly less often by lower income group subjects than by their middle and higher income group counterparts (λ^2 (2) = 8.94; p < .05). The 20 percent discount led to an additional sale of twenty-two bulbs, with no difference on frequency of bulb purchasing being evident among the three income groups (λ^2 (2) = 2.32; n. s.).

Finally, a significantly (λ^2 (2) = 7.47; p < .05) higher percentage of higher income subjects (11 out of 24) and middle income subjects (16 out of 40) purchased bulbs on the Total measure than did lower income subjects (4 out of 29).

Data sets for Studies 1 and 2 were merged to compare their findings directly. Significantly (t = 3.41; p < .01) more bulbs were sold overall to Study 2 subjects ($\overline{X}$ = .78 bulbs) than to Study 1 subjects ($\overline{X}$ = .22 bulbs). This might suggest that the group information session led to greater sales of bulbs in Study 2. However, there was also a relationship between level of education and number of bulbs purchased overall (r = .41; p < .01) and the education level of Study 2 subjects (mean of about grade 14) was higher (albeit, nonsignificantly) than subjects who took part in Study 1 (mean of about grade 12). Thus, our claim that the group information presentation might have been responsible for the greater bulb sales in Study 2 must be tempered somewhat by this rival hypothesis.

Taken together with Study 1, the present data suggest that higher income subjects will purchase high efficiency light bulbs when offered the information of their ecological importance and long–term economic superiority to standard incandescent bulbs. The major effect of the latter incentives (free trial use and a 20 percent discount) is to bring the participation of middle and lower income level subjects closer to the level of participation of their higher income group counterparts. In Appendix C, I will demonstrate why additional incentives that enable poorer people to participate more equally in energy efficiency programs carry an important *moral* significance. This is due to the fact that while incentive programs appear to bear no negative consequences for people who choose not to participate, this is *not* in reality the case. Any incentive program that does not achieve equal participation by members of all income groups (which is, in fact, the current state of virtually all utility-sponsored programs) represents an instance of economic discrimination—in spite of the red herring that all income groups are treated fairly since all are offered the same monetary incentives.

The present studies might suggest that far larger numbers of sales occur when people discuss the economic and ecological benefits of high efficiency lighting in group settings. This could represent good news to psychologists, as no other professional group is better trained or more frequently involved in offering group interventions than are psychologists (Fuhriman and Burlingame 1990). Group process researchers might now attempt to tease out the exact factors that maximize the impact of these groups, and consider further questions such as the impact of follow-up group sessions and extending the groups' momentum into action in other domains of ecological concern (e.g., recycling, birth control, tree planting, political action).

The Global Action Plan (84 Yerry Hill Road, Woodstock, NY 12498) offers materials through a Household Ecoteam Program whereby you and your neighbors can form a group to systematically tackle six areas (reduce your garbage; improve home water efficiency; improve home energy efficiency; improve transportation efficiency; be an eco-wise consumer; and empower others through household, workplace, and community action) over a six month period. These changes will make each group member's lifestyle more "Earth friendly."

The two studies herein fit well with the literature in ecological psychology (see Stern 1992a, 1992b; Stokals and Altman 1987) as they represent applied, experimental studies of how energy-saving devices might be put into service. Replacing inefficient technologies is apparently a superior strategy to simply exhorting consumers to try to use less electricity each day, as voluntary conservation efforts often wane over time. However, an extremely efficient technology continues to save electricity for years regardless of possible changes in motivation and awareness by the consumer.

APPENDIX C

CAN YOU AFFORD NOT TO CONSERVE ELECTRICITY?

Electric rates are determined by two factors: 1) the continuing costs of producing and delivering electricity (i.e., workers' wages, the prices of fuels, equipment costs such as transmission wires, computers, repair vehicles, etc.); and 2) costs associated with increasing the utility's capacity to supply electricity. With regard to the continuing costs of producing and delivering electricity, if workers' wages increase, or if the costs of coal or oil increases, those changes would result in higher electricity rates. Similarly, if labor costs were lowered, or if fuel costs declined, those cost savings would result in lower utility rates. The relationship of the continuing costs of providing electricity to the rates you pay for the commodity are rather straightforward.

However, the costs associated with increasing a utility's generating capacity are less obvious. As a simplification strategy, let's consider the situation of my neighbor Mary and me—but remember that we each will stand for half of the customers that our utility serves. Imagine that Mary and I have equal residential electricity needs (i.e., 10,000 kW. hrs./year), and that our electricity cost is $.06/kW. hr. Next imagine that I&M projected that our need for electricity would increase by 20 percent over the next five years, and that additional generating capacity would be required to meet our demand for power. I&M could petition the Indiana Utility Regulatory Commission for permission to build another power plant to meet the projected increase in demand. (This is *supply-side* management—the utility increases its capacity to supply power in order to maintain a supply-demand balance.) Along with permission to build the power plant, I&M also expects to be allowed to enter the cost of the plant (plus a reasonable rate of return on its investment) into

Table C-1

	Yearly bill, 1992	1997 20% increased consumption by both	1997 differential consumption
George	10,000 × .06 = $600	12,000 × .07 = $840	10,000 × .07 = $700
Mary	10,000 × .06 = $600	12,000 × .07 = $840	14,000 × .07 = $980
Totals	20,000 kW hrs. $1,200	24,000 kW hrs. $1,680	24,000 kwW hrs. $1,680

its rate structure. Thus, let's imagine that the electricity rate went from \$.06/kW. hr. to \$.07/kW. hr. over five years *due solely* to the cost of the new power plant. (For simplicity, let's assume the continuing costs of producing and delivering the electricity remained unchanged over the five-year period.) Table C-1 shows Mary's and my yearly electric bills under different circumstances.

The first column shows that both Mary and I paid \$600 for electricity in 1992. Since (in the middle column) we were equally responsible for the 20 percent consumption increase, it is proper that each of our bills are increased by \$240 in order to compensate I&M for its investment in the new power plant. However, in the third column, I (presumably through heroic conservation efforts) have kept my 1997 consumption equal to my 1992 consumption—and still my bill increased from 1992 to 1997 by \$100. But Mary's consumption has increased by 40 percent (making I&M's projected average increase correct), and thus she pays the lion's share \$380 (or \$980 less \$600) of the money required to increase generating capacity. It is unfair, you might claim, that my bill should increase by \$100 simply because Mary consumed more electricity in 1997 than in 1992. In fact, I&M tries to modulate such inequities by charging customers different rates based upon their peak consumption. Thus, if I&M charged me \$.06/kW. hr. (because my peak consumption was rather low) and they charged Mary \$.077/kW. hr. (because her peak consumption was higher) then she would pay for the entire rate increase caused by the need to generate more electricity.

Contrast that scenario with a different situation, where a utility attempts to meet projected supply-demand imbalances by investing its money into programs that *reduce* the demand for its electricity (more precisely, the utility attempts to shave the peaks off its demand curve) which will eliminate its need to build additional generating capacity. By all accounts (see Gillings and Chamberlain 1988), demand-side management represents the wave of the future as ever-increasing supply solutions to supply-demand imbalances have catastrophic effects on the environment. Thus, I&M now offers cash incentives to residential consumers who purchase geothermal heating and cooling units, upgrade insulation, purchase energy efficient major appliances, purchase high efficiency lighting, and take part in other incentive programs. Paralleling the earlier example, imagine that I&M now charges $.06/kW. hr.; anticipates a 20 percent demand increase over five years if no systematic conservation programs are initiated; that a 4000 kW. hrs. reduction of demand through conservation incentive programs will require that Mary and I pay a total of $1,680 in 1997 rather than $1,200 as in 1992 (thus, we assume that a 4000 kW. hrs. increase in supply can be purchased at the same cost as a 4000 kW. hrs. reduction through conservation); that the continuing costs of producing and delivery will remain unchanged over the five-year period; and finally (since conservation incentive programs are voluntary) that half of I&M's customers will participate in the incentive programs.

The purpose of this exercise is to determine (once again) who will bear the costs of demand-side incentive programs under various combinations of conditions (i.e., consumers' increase demand equally or differentially). There is some realism to this example in that in the last two years I have accepted cash incentives from I&M for the installation of a geothermal heater and air conditioner and for the purchase of energy efficient compact fluorescent light bulbs. My neighbor Mary has not availed herself of either incentive program. But the costs of these incentive programs will enter I&M's rate base, just as if the utility had built a new power plant to meet the anticipated supply-demand imbalance. Who will pay for demand-side programs? Mary or me?

As in the first example, Table C-2 reveals that Mary and I each pay $600/year in 1992. Again, in the second column, our normal consumption for 1997 would have increased by 20 percent (through purchases of computers, freezers, additions to our homes, etc.). But my total electricity consumption is reduced by 4000 kW. hrs. due to my geothermal unit and the light bulbs which consume only 20–30 percent the electricity of the standard incandescent bulbs they

Table C-2

	Yearly bill, 1992	1997 20% increased consumption by both	1997 differential consumption
George	10,000 × .06 = $600	12,000 kW. hrs. −4.000 Conservation Devices 8,000 × .084 = $672	10,000 kW. hrs. −4.000 Conservation Devices 6,000 × .084 = $504
Mary	10,000 × .06 = $600	12,000 × .084 = $1008	14,000 × .084 = $1176
Totals	20,000 kW. hrs. $1,200	20,000 kW. hrs. $1,680	20,000 kW. hrs. $1,680

replaced. So now I use 8,000 kW. hrs. each year, and Mary uses 12,000 kW. hrs. The supply-demand balance is maintained, but at a 20,000 kW. hrs. level for the two of us rather than at the 24,000 kW. hrs. level as in Table C-1. The big winner with demand-side programs is obviously the earth—which will have to contend with significantly less greenhouse gases (carbon dioxide), acid rain (sulphur dioxide), and smog (nitrous oxide) because of I&M's conservation program.

But what of Mary and me? Do we absorb the costs of demand-side solutions in exactly the same proportions as occurred in the supply-side solution depicted in Table C-1? The answer is a dramatic "No"! With supply solutions the consumer has no choice—when the utility decides to add to its capacity, rates go up for everyone. But demand-side programs are voluntary. Even if Mary declines to participate in incentive programs, the program's costs show up in her utility rates—just as all of us, whether we approve or not, must pay part of the cost of a new nuclear power plant, if that's how I&M and the Indiana Utility Regulatory Commission decide to deal with a particular anticipated supply-demand imbalance. When Mary decides to say "no thank you" to the demand-side incentive program, she agrees (although without knowing she is doing so) to subsidize a substantial portion of the program's costs. Here's how it happens.

In column two of Table C-2, I&M must generate $1,680 of payments from Mary and me (as in Table C-1) but now it must obtain the additional revenues on 20,000 kW. hrs. of consumption (rather than 24,000 kW. hrs. as in Table C-1). Thus, instead of going from

$.06/kW. hr. to $.07/kW. hr. as in the first solution, in the demand-side solution the rates must increase from $.06/kW. hr. to $.084/kW. hr. In the first example, Mary's and my bills both increased from $600/year to $840/year. In the demand–side, conservation solution, my bill increases from $600/yr. to $672/yr., while poor Mary's bill goes from $600/yr. to $1,008/yr.

Recall that in the third column, I hold my electricity consumption constant while Mary allows her electricity use to increase by 40 percent from 1992 to 1997. But in Table C-2, I accept the demand-side incentive, but Mary declines. In this instance, my utility bill declines from $600 to $504, whereas poor, poor Mary's bill almost doubles in going from $600 to $1,176. Thus, when she says "no" to demand-side incentive programs, Mary decides to bear the lion's share of the cost of those programs! But again, since exact rates are based upon peak consumption, and since her peak demand will not be lowered by conservation devices, the actual discrepancy between my cost and Mary's cost will be even greater than shown in columns 2 and 3 of Table C-2.

The point of this exercise is simple. Given the structure of our society (and the current state of our world's ecology), we must implement demand-side conservation solutions, rather than the standard response of increasing electricity supply to rectify supply-demand imbalances. But the people who say "no" to demand-side incentive programs commit themselves (usually unknowingly) to bearing the lion's share of the cost of those programs. It is only when all of us say "yes" to demand-side incentive programs that the costs of those programs are borne equitably. I like my neighbor, Mary. I don't want to see her get soaked. We'll all feel much better when each of us does our small part to save the earth. So, come on Mary, can you really afford *not* to take I&M's money to conserve electricity?

The problem of who pays for demand-side incentive programs becomes a moral issue when poor people say "no" because they do not possess the financial resources to pay the additional money needed to qualify for the incentive. Programs like "Heat for the Poor" collect donations from local individuals, businesses, and utilities to help poor families pay their heating bills in winter. Similar programs could be started to pay a percentage of poor families' costs of participating in demand-side incentive programs.

However, my neighbor Mary could easily afford the money to avail herself of the incentive program. Her need was for greater awareness of the issues at stake and reliable information from credible sources (not people who are currently trying to sell her products). This is where public service announcements in the local media by disinterested parties (e.g., university professors) and governmental resources (e.g., Department of Energy, Environmental Protection Agency, Better Business Bureau) can offer solid advice from knowledgeable individuals who do not stand to make a profit from the sale. Finally, all of the above resources routinely answer questions, so you and Mary need not wait for a public service announcement in the newspaper. Mary can initiate a search for information herself. The manufacturers, distributors, and installers of the instruments in question are happy to supply the basic technological information. Your local utility and governmental agencies will then help you to conduct disinterested analyses of your options.

CALVIN AND HOBBES

BILL WATTERSON

REFERENCES

Albee, G. W. 1977. "The Protestant Ethic, Sex, and Psychotherapy." *American Psychologist* 32: 150–161.

Anonymous. 1991. "Flashing Neon Lights." Term paper submitted for a course on "Ideas, Values and Images."

Archer, D., T. F. Pettigrew, and E. Aronson. 1992. "Making Research Apply: High Stakes Public Policy in a Regulatory Environment." *American Psychologist* 47: 1233–1236.

Becker, E. 1971. *The Birth and Death of Meaning.* New York: The Free Press.

Becker, E. 1973. *The Denial of Death.* New York: The Free Press.

Bellah, R. N., R. Madsen, W. M. Sullivan, A. Swindler, and S. M. Tipton. 1985. *Habits of the Heart: Individualism and Commitment in American Life.* New York: Harper & Row.

Boulding, K. E. 1966. "The Economics of the Coming Spaceship Earth." In *Environmental Quality in a Growing Economy,* published for Resources for the Future. Baltimore: Johns Hopkins University Press.

Brown, L. R. 1991. "The New World Order." In *State of the World: 1991,* ed. L. R. Brown. New York: Norton. Pp. 3–16.

Brown, L. R. 1994. "Facing Food Insecurity." In *State of the World: 1994,* ed. L. R. Brown. New York: Norton. Pp. 177–198.

Brown, L. R., C. Flavin, and S. Postel. 1990. "Picturing a Sustainable Society." In *State of the World: 1990,* ed. L. R. Brown. New York: Norton.

Brown, L. R., C. Flavin, and S. Postel. 1991. *Saving the Planet: How to Shape an Environmentally Sustainable Global Economy.* New York: Norton.

Burke, J. 1987. *After the Warming.* New York: Ambrose Video Publishing Company.

Chiras, D. D. 1992. *Lessons from Nature: Learning to Live Sustainably on the Earth.* Washington, D.C.: Island Press.

Chiras, D. D. (Ed.) 1995. *Voices for the Earth.* Boulder, Colo.: Johnson Books.

Clawson, G. 1923. *The Richest Man in Babylon.* New York: Nal Penguin.

Coleman, S., and N. Hull-Mast. 1992. *Can't Buy Me Love.* Minneapolis: Fairview Press.

Corporation for Public Broadcasting. 1990. *Race to Save the Planet.* Santa Barbara, Calif.: Annenberg Collection.

Cotkin, G. 1990. *William James, Public Philosopher.* Baltimore: Johns Hopkins University Press.

Durning, A. T. 1992. *How Much Is Enough? The Consumer Society and the Future of the Earth.* New York: Norton.

Ehrlich, P. R. 1968. *The Population Bomb.* New York: Ballantine.

Ehrlich, P. R., and A. H. Ehrlich. 1990. *The Population Explosion.* New York: Simon & Schuster.

Ehrlich, P. R., and A. H. Ehrlich. 1991. *Healing the Planet.* Reading, Mass.: Addison Wesley.

Ellis, A. 1994. *Reason and Emotion in Psychotherapy.* New York: Carol Publishing Group.

Freud, S. 1936. *The Problem of Anxiety.* New York: Norton. Originally published in 1926.

Frontline. 1994. *The Diamond Empire.* Washington, D.C.: The Corporation for Public Broadcasting.

Fuhriman, A., and G. M. Burlingame. 1990. "Group Therapy." *The Counseling Psychologist* (whole issue) 18: 5–139.

Garbarino, J. 1995. *Raising Children in a Socially Toxic Environment.* San Francisco: Jossey-Bass.

Gardner, G. T., and P. C. Stern. 1996. *Environmental Problems and Human Behavior.* New York: Allyn & Bacon.

Gellings, C. W., and J. H. Chamberlain. 1988. *Demand-side Management: Concepts and Methods.* Lilburn, Ga.: Fairmont Press.

Glendenning, C. 1995. "Technology, Trauma, and the Wild." In *Ecopsychology,* ed. T. Roszak, M. E. Gomes, and A.D. Kanner. San Francisco: Sierra Club Books.

Gore, A. 1992. *Earth in the Balance: Ecology and the Human Spirit.* Boston: Houghton Mifflin.

Hardin, G. 1964. *Population, Evolution, and Birth Control.* San Francisco: W. H. Freeman.

Hardin, G. 1968. "The Tragedy of the Commons." *Science* 162: 1243–1248.

Hardin, G. 1993. *Living within Limits: Ecology, Economics, and Population Taboos.* New York: Oxford University Press.

Hawken, P. 1993. *The Ecology of Commerce.* New York: Harper Collins.

Henderson, H. 1981. *The Politics of the Solar Alternatives to Economics Age.* Garden City, N.Y.: Anchor/Doubleday.

Herrnstein, R. J. 1990. "Rational Choice Theory: Necessary But Not Sufficient." *American Psychologist* 45: 356–367.

Howard, G. S. 1992a. "Where Were You When the Earth Was Dying?" *Contemporary Psychology* 37: 1141–1143.

Howard, G. S. 1992b. "Why William James Might Be Considered the Founder of the Scientist-Practitioner Model." *The Counseling Psychologist* 21: 118–135.

Howard, G. S. 1993a. "Thoughts on Saving Our Planet: Political, Economic, Cultural, and Bureaucratic Impediments to Ecological Activism." *The Counseling Psychologist* 21: 596–616.

Howard, G. S. 1993b. "Impaled upon the Horns of Faith and Reason." *America* 168: 12–15.

Howard, G. S. 1994. "Reflections on Change in Science and Religion." *International Journal of Psychology and Religion* 4: 127–143.

Howard, G. S. 1996. *Understanding Human Nature: An Owner's Manual.* Notre Dame, Ind.: Academic Publications.

Howard, G. S., E. Delgado, D. Miller, and S. Gubbins. 1993. "Transforming Values into Actions: Ecological Preservation through Energy Conservation." *The Counseling Psychologist* 21: 581–595.

Howard, G. S., and S. E. Maxwell. 1983. "Linked Rater's Judgments: A More Sensitive Index of Change." *Evaluation Review* 6: 140–146.

Howard, G. S., F. H. Obledo, D. A. Cole, and S. E. Maxwell. 1983. "Linked Judgments: A Solution to Problems of Statistical Conclusion Validity." *Applied Psychological Measurement* 7: 57–62.

James, W. 1897. *The Will to Believe.* New York: Longmans Green.

James, W. 1899. *Talks to Teachers on Psychology.* New York: Henry Holt.

James, W. 1920. *The Letters of William James.* 2 vols. Boston: Atlantic Monthly Press.

Kempton, W., J. M. Darley, and P. C. Stern. 1992. "Psychological Research for the New Energy Problems: Strategies and Opportunities." *American Psychologist* 47: 1213–1223.

Lazarus, R. S. 1974. *The Riddle of Man.* Englewood Cliffs, N.J.: Prentice Hall.

Lockard, J. S., and D. L. Paulhus. (Eds.) 1988. *Self-deception: An Adaptive Mechanism?* Englewood Cliffs, N.J.: Prentice Hall.

Lopate, P. 1995. *The Art of the Personal Essay.* New York: Anchor/ Doubleday.

Malthus, T. 1798. "An Essay on the Principle of Population." Reprinted in *Population, Evolution and Birth Control: A Collage of Controversial Readings,* ed. G. Hardin. San Francisco: Freeman, 1964.

Meadows, D. H., D. L. Meadows, and J. Randers. 1992. *Beyond the Limits.* White River Junction, Vt.: Chelsea Green.

Miller, G. T. 1993. *Environmental Science: Sustaining the Earth.* 4th ed. Belmont, Calif.: Wadsworth.

Miller, J. 1993. "The St. Joe County Solid Waste Dilemma." *Around the Bend* 7: 1–2.

Ornstein, R., and P. Ehrlich. 1989. *New World/New Mind.* New York: Doubleday.

Pelletier, K. R. 1977. *Mind as Healer, Mind as Slayer.* New York: Delacorte.

Perlman, J. E. 1990. "A Dual Strategy for Deliberate Social Change in Cities." *Cities* 3–15.

Population Institute. 1991. *Annual Report.* Washington, D.C.

Population Reference Bureau. 1989. *Global Population Trends.* Washington, D.C.

Postel, S. 1992. "Denial in the Decisive Decade." In *State of the World: 1992,* ed. L. R. Brown. New York: Norton. Pp. 3–8.

Robbins, L. G. 1989. *Uncommon Cents: Benjamin Franklin's Secrets to Achieving Personal Financial Success.* Salt Lake City, Utah: Franklin International Institute.

Rogers, C. R. 1961. *On Becoming a Person: A Therapist's View of Psychotherapy.* Boston: Houghton Mifflin.

Roszak, T. 1992. *The Voice of the Earth.* New York: Simon & Schuster.

Roszak, T., M. E. Gomes, and A.D. Kanner. (Eds.) 1995. *Ecopsychology: Restoring the Earth, Healing the Mind.* San Francisco: Sierra Club Books.

Sampson, E. E. 1988. "The Debate on Individualism: Indigenous Psychologies of the Individual and Their Role in Personal and Societal Functioning." *American Psychologist* 43: 115–122.

Savitt, W., and P. Bottorf. 1995. *Global Development: A Reference Handbook.* Santa Barbara, Calif.: ABC-CLIO.

Schelling, T. C. 1978. *Micromotives and Macrobehavior.* New York: Norton.

Schmidheiny, S. 1995. Changing Course: A Global Business Perspective on Development and the Environment. In *Voices for the Earth,* ed. D. D. Chiras. Boulder, Colo.: Johnson Books.

Schultz, D. 1977. *Growth Psychology: Models for the Healthy Personality.* New York: Van Nostrand.

Schumacher, E. F. 1973. *Small Is Beautiful.* New York: Harper & Row.

Schwartz, B. 1986. *The Battle for Human Nature.* New York: Norton.

Shapiro, A. L. 1992. *We're Number One: Where America Stands—and Falls—in the New World Order.* New York: Random House.

Shepard, P. 1995. "Nature and Madness." In *Ecopsychology,* ed. T. Roszak, M. E. Gomes, and A.D. Kanner. San Francisco: Sierra Club Books.

Stern, P. C. 1992a. "Psychological Dimensions of Global Environmental Change." *Annual Review of Psychology* 43: 269–302.

Stern, P. C. 1992b. "What Psychology Knows about Energy Conservation." *American Psychologist* 47: 1224–1232.

Stevens, W. K. 1995. "Ecosystems Identified as Critical or Endangered." *South Bend Tribune,* February 14, A5.

Stokels, D., and I. Altman. (Eds.) 1987. *Handbook of Environmental Psychology.* New York: Wiley.

Tapinos, G., and P. T. Piotrow. 1978. *Six Billion People: Demographic Dilemmas and World Politics.* New York: McGraw-Hill.

Weber, S. 1992. *Population Growth.* Fact sheet distributed by Zero Population Growth, 11400 16th St. N.W. #320, Washington, D.C. 20036.

Willems, E. P. 1974. "Behavioral Technology and Behavioral Ecology." *Journal of Applied Behavior Analysis* 7: 151–165.

Wilson, E. O. 1992. *The Diversity of Life.* New York: Norton.

ABOUT THE AUTHOR

George S. Howard is a professor in the Department of Psychology at the University of Notre Dame where he has served as Director of Graduate Studies and twice served as chairman of the department. Professor Howard serves as a faculty fellow in Notre Dame's Urban Institute, the Reilly Center for Science Technology and Values, and the Kroc Institute for International Peace Studies. He received a doctorate in counseling psychology in 1975 from Southern Illinois University in Carbondale, Illinois. His research has focused upon theoretical, methodological, and philosophical problems in applied areas of psychological research such as counseling, clinical, educational, industrial/organizational, and ecological psychology. A fellow of six divisions of the American Psychological Association, he currently serves as president of both the Division of Theoretical and Philosophical Psychology and the Division of Humanistic Psychology. He is the author of six other books, and over one hundred and fifty book chapters and articles in professional journals. He and his wife, Nancy Gulanick, are the parents of two sons, John Gulanick and Gregory Howard.